The Handwriting on the Wall

Volume 2

BY DR. DAVID JEREMIAH

Turning Point

Published by Walk Thru the Bible Ministries, Atlanta, Georgia.

Unless otherwise indicated, Scripture verses quoted are taken from the NEW KING JAMES VERSION.
Copyright © 1979, 1980, 1982 by Thomas Nelson, Inc.
Used by permission.

Printed in the United States of America.

Contents

About
Dr. David Jeremiah
and Turning Point
Ministries

Dr. David Jeremiah is the founder of Turning Point Ministries, a ministry committed to providing Christians with sound Bible teaching relevant to today's changing times through radio broadcasts, audiocassette series, and books. Dr. Jeremiah's "common sense" teaching on such topics as family, stress, the New Age, and Biblical prophecy forms the foundation of Turning Point Ministries.

Dr. Jeremiah is the senior pastor of Shadow Mountain Community Church in El Cajon near San Diego, California, where he also serves as President of Christian Heritage College. He and his wife Donna have four children.

In 1982, Dr. Jeremiah wanted to bring the same solid teaching to San Diego television that he shared weekly with his congregation. Shortly thereafter, Turning Point expanded its ministry to radio. Dr. Jeremiah's inspiring messages are currently broadcast weekly from over 250 national and international radio stations.

Because Dr. Jeremiah desires to know his listening audience, he travels nationwide holding "A Night of Encouragement" radio rallies that touch the hearts and lives of many. According to Dr. Jeremiah, "At some point in time everyone reaches a turning point, and for every person that moment is unique, an experience to hold onto forever. There's so much changing in today's world, sometimes it's difficult to always choose the right path. Turning Point Ministries offers real people an understanding of God's Word, as well as the opportunity to make a difference in their lives."

Dr. Jeremiah has authored eight books including *Escape the Coming Night*, *The Handwriting on the Wall*, *Exposing the Myths of Parenthood*, *Turning Toward Joy* (Philippians), and *Turning Toward Integrity* (James).

About This Study Guide

The purpose of this Turning Point study guide is to reinforce Dr. David Jeremiah's dynamic, in-depth teaching on *The Handwriting on the Wall* and aid the reader in applying Biblical truth to his or her daily life. This study guide is designed to be used in conjunction with Dr. Jeremiah's *The Handwriting on the Wall* audio-cassette series, but it may also be used by itself for personal or group Bible study.

Structure of the Lessons

Each lesson is based on one of the tapes in *The Handwriting on the Wall* audiocassette series and focuses on a specific passage in the Bible. Each lesson is composed of the following elements:

- ## Outline

    The outline at the beginning of the lesson gives a clear, concise picture of the passage being studied and provides a helpful framework for readers as they listen to Dr. Jeremiah's teaching.

- ## Overview

    The overview summarizes Dr. Jeremiah's teaching on the passage being studied in the lesson. Readers should refer to the passage in their own Bibles as they study the overview.

- ## Application

    This section contains a variety of questions designed to help readers dig deeper into the lesson and the Scriptures, and to apply the lesson to their daily lives. For Bible study groups or Sunday school classes, these questions will provide a springboard for group discussion and interaction.

Did You Know?

This section presents a fun fact, historical note, or insight which adds a point of interest to the preceding lesson.

Using This Guide for Group Study

The lessons in this study guide are suitable for Sunday school classes, small-group studies, elective Bible studies, or home Bible study groups. Each person in the group should have his or her own study guide.

When possible, the study guide should be used with the corresponding tape series. You may wish to assign the study guide as homework prior to the meeting of the group and then use the meeting time to listen to the tape and discuss the lesson.

For Continuing Study

A complete catalog of Dr. Jeremiah's materials for personal and group study is available through Turning Point Ministries. To obtain a catalog, additional study guides, or more information about Turning Point, call 1-800-947-1993 or write to: Turning Point Ministries, P.O. Box 3838, San Diego, CA 92163.

Dr. Jeremiah's "Turning Point" radio broadcast is currently heard on more than 250 national and international radio stations. Contact your local Christian radio station or Turning Point Ministries for program times in your area.

The Handwriting on the Wall

Volume 2

INTRODUCTION

Once upon a time, in a land far, far away. . ." These well-known words almost seem appropriate as we begin this study in the Book of Daniel. This book of the Bible tells amazing stories of a fiery furnace, a lions' den, and even mysterious handwriting on the wall. But Daniel is no fairy tale; it is completely God's Word. And the book doesn't conclude with a pat "happily ever after" ending. Visions of tribulation and terror in the end times reveal a less than ideal future for many people of the world.

But take heart! For Daniel is full of encouraging news. Through the lives of faithful believers such as Shadrach, Meshach, Abed-Nego and Daniel, God proves His own power to defend and deliver. Even though God does allow scary trials to afflict His own, He never abandons them.

And if you have ever wanted to see the future, the prophecies and interpreted dreams in Daniel offer a glimpse. Daniel is the first apocalyptic writer in the Bible. His writings convey prophecies through signs and symbols. This study will help you to interpret the meaning of these prophecies. As the mysteries are clarified, you'll also find guidance for what you can do now to prepare for what is to come.

Daniel, along with corresponding passages in the book of Revelation, also gives insight into the character of God and the Kingdom of Jesus Christ. Glimpsing the majestic throne room of glory is a marvelous contrast to the earthly power wielded by the Antichrist. Realizing that God's kingdom is eternal, and worldly kingdoms only temporal, is a soul-inspiring relief.

Just who is this Antichrist who will assume leadership in the world in its end days? How will he come to power . . . gain control . . . persecute Christians? This study guide probes the characteristics of, and historical role played by, this ungodly character. As you learn more about the Antichrist, you can plan your own strategy for avoiding his traps of deceit.

Where will the Church be when the tribulation period begins? Basing his interpretations on a consistent interpretation of Scripture, Dr. Jeremiah explains his "pre-tribulational view." In other words, the Church will be safe with the Lord before the world undergoes final judgment and destruction.

Christ Himself talks about the end times with His disciples, as recorded in the Book of Matthew. He teaches the disciples what will happen before His Kingdom on earth is established. The prophecies He relays reassure believers that God is in control of the future, and that He will come again one day.

Daniel was given two visions. Portions of the second one, as recorded in chapter eight, have been fulfilled already in history. We will see in hindsight how literally the prophecies came to pass. Other parts have yet to be accomplished, but we can be assured that they will be in God's due time. And we need to be prepared— for the prophecy yet to pass is of the coming of the Antichrist.

This Antichrist will be a powerful, cunning leader of the people, destined to do evil and destructive in his reign. Imagine the worst atrocities of history, in terms of cruelty toward and slaughter of humanity, then multiply them beyond your wildest imaginings. That gives you a clue to the identity of the man who will set off the tribulation. Yet God will ultimately remain in control. One day Jesus will return to earth to cast the Antichrist into hell.

As He did when saving Daniel from the crushing jaws of the lions, so He will when saving the world from the Antichrist. God will prove Himself faithful. He will protect His own and punish the wicked. Let this exciting news be your impetus to work even harder today, tomorrow, and every day until He returns, to further the Kingdom of God in your own world.

Daniel in the Lions' Den

Daniel 6:14-28

*In this lesson we will see how Daniel was
delivered from death.*

OUTLINE

As we look at the story of Daniel in the lions' den, we will see what has happened to some who persisted in their faith. We will also learn four principles about lions' dens in our own lives.

- I. Daniel Preferred by Darius
- II. Daniel Persecuted by His Enemies
- III. Daniel Persistent in His Testimony
- IV. Daniel Protected by His God
  - A. The Displeasure of the King
  - B. The Deliverance of Daniel to the Den
  - C. The Depression of the King
  - D. The Deliverance of Daniel in the Den
- V. Daniel Proved by His God
- VI. Daniel and Practical Applications
  - A. The Probability of the Lions' Den
  - B. The Promise of the Lions' Den
  - C. The Purpose of the Lions' Den
  - D. The Prosperity of the Lions' Den

OVERVIEW

Under the fearful persecution of Nero, the Christians of Rome went through fiery trials. Multitudes of them were burned at the stake. The very streets at night were ghastly to behold, because they were lit up with human torches made out of the Christians who were being burned alive.

In the Polish romance, *Quo Vadis*, Peter is shown fleeing the persecution with a little band of fugitive Christians. He came face to face with Jesus, who was walking toward the city. The Lord said to Peter, "Where are you going?"

Peter asked Him the same question, and the Lord said, "I'm going back to Rome to be crucified again because my servant Peter has turned his back on the cross."

Peter answered, "Not so, Lord. I will go back and gladly die for thee."

Tradition tells us Peter let them nail him to the cross, upside down so he would not be compared to his Lord, trusting that his blood would be the seed of the church and his sacrifice would send the message of Truth further than his living speech would carry it.

I don't know the truth of the first part of the story, but I do believe Peter was crucified upside down because he felt himself unworthy to be crucified in the same manner as his Lord. And as I read the story, I was reminded that the heritage of our faith is founded upon the sacrifice and courage of people like Peter and Daniel.

Daniel was wonderfully delivered from death. Peter paid for his faith with his life. Believing God does not necessarily guarantee that you will not be eaten by lions, but in Daniel's case, deliverance was part of God's plan.

Daniel Preferred by Darius

The Scripture records that when King Darius came into the Medo-Persian rule, he chose Daniel out of all the men in his kingdom and made him Prime Minister. He was one of three presidents, but he was above the other two. Under him were all of the 120 princes that governed throughout that great area. He was preferred "because an excellent spirit was in him" (Daniel 6:3). He had God within him.

Daniel Persecuted by His Enemies

Daniel had no sooner taken that responsibility when he was persecuted by his enemies. They determined to get Daniel. They were jealous and envious of him. He was a foreigner who had been elevated above them, and they hated him. He was also an honest man. They were not able to traffic in corruption as they were accustomed.

They tried first to indict him for some fault in his life, but they could find nothing wrong with him. In his professional life he was clean. In his personal life he was absolutely spotless. They determined the only way they could get Daniel in trouble was to accuse him in the matter of his religion. They observed that Daniel was very regular in his prayer life. So they determined to catch him in a habit they knew he would never break.

Daniel Persistent in His Testimony

When they had the law passed that King Darius was to be god for a month and anybody who refused to bow down before him would be thrown into the den of lions, Daniel was caught in the trap. The king was actually the one caught because, when he agreed to the law, he didn't know Daniel would be the one condemned.

Daniel didn't change at all. He kept right on doing what he had always done. He persisted. In the text it says over and over that Daniel was a persistent man of God. In this passage, twice the king said to him, "Daniel, you are the guy who continually serves his God." That was his testimony. He persisted in his faith.

Daniel Protected by His God

The Displeasure of the King

When the king heard about Daniel disobeying the commandment and praying to his own God, the king was very displeased. He was not displeased with Daniel; he was displeased with himself because he had been tricked. He didn't want to hurt Daniel.

King Darius had his heart set on delivering Daniel. The Bible says he worked until the sun went down to try and find a way out for Daniel. But under Persian law, when a person was convicted of a crime and the sentence was passed, the sentence was carried out on that same day. As soon as the sentence was passed there was no opportunity for redress or appeal.

The Deliverance of Daniel to the Den

You have probably seen pictures of Daniel standing in the lions' den in quiet contemplation, with two or three lions looking at him in awe. You might want to adjust your picture of what happened that night. We find out later on in the text that those who accused Daniel were thrown into the den, and they were devoured before they hit the floor. How many people were there? Over a hundred princes and others, plus their families. How many lions would it take to eat that many people before they hit the floor of the lions' den? A lot of lions!

One writer described Daniel sliding to the floor of the den and the big lions bounding up, then stopping short. "The initial roars died away as they formed a solid phalanx and looked toward this man as he stood in their den within their easy reach. There was some snorting and a little whining, and some of them turned around and went back to their caverns." Two lion cubs and their mother came and lay beside Daniel "as though to give him warmth and protection in the chilly dungeon."

The Depression of the King

When King Darius went back to his palace, he could not sleep or eat or be diverted. They couldn't find any way for the king to get his mind off of his troubled heart about his friend in the lions' den. The king was not only losing a friend, he was also losing his number one administrator for the whole kingdom. Even though Darius had not deliberately delivered Daniel to the lions' den, he was responsible because his own vanity had caused it to happen.

The Deliverance of Daniel in the Den

The king got up early the next morning and hurried to the den. In a lamenting voice, he cried out, "Daniel, servant of the living God, has your God, whom you serve continually, been able to deliver you from the lions?" (Daniel 6:20). Earlier, when they had put Daniel in the lions' den, the king said to him, "Your God, whom you serve continually, He will deliver you" (v. 16). That's the kind of pious thing you say to someone who is hurting, even when you don't believe it yourself. Obviously the king didn't believe it, because he asked if what he said had happened.

Daniel responded, "My God sent His angel and shut the lions' mouths, so that they have not hurt me" (v. 22). The rationale for his deliverance was that he was innocent.

The king reacted with gladness and commanded them to take Daniel out of the den. Daniel was not hurt at all, and the reason given for this in the Scripture was, "because he believed in his God" (v. 23).

The history of what God has done in a miraculous way from the beginning of Christianity right up to modern day is wrapped up in what God does for somebody who believes in his God. It wasn't because Daniel was special. He wasn't one of God's pets. It wasn't because he was elected or foreordained or predestined. It was because Daniel believed in his God. He wasn't any different from us except in the measure of his faith in his almighty God.

Daniel Proved by His God

Verse twenty-four is a sorry story of the paganism of the Medo-Persian empire. It says, "And the king gave the command, and they brought those men who had accused Daniel, and they cast them into the den of lions—them, their children, and their wives; and the lions overpowered them, and broke all their bones in pieces before they ever came to the bottom of the den."

Sometimes people try to explain the story of Daniel by saying the lions weren't very hungry that day, or that Daniel hid and the lions couldn't find him. But these were hungry, ravenous, ferocious lions.

All of those who persecuted Daniel were themselves persecuted. I believe when people reach out to touch God's anointed, God often touches them.

Daniel and Practical Applications

The Probability of the Lions' Den

The nature of the Christian faith marks all of us for the lions. We are out of step with the world around us, and that's why we are always in jeopardy of the lions' den. Earlier in the Book of Daniel, Shadrach, Meshach and Abed-Nego were standing when everyone else was kneeling. Now everybody else is standing and Daniel is kneeling. Shadrach, Meshach and Abed-Nego were out of step with their times. Daniel was out of step with his times.

God delivered them. But He delivered them through the fiery furnace and through the lions' den. There was no attempt on the part of God to withhold them from the pressure of certain death. It will be like that for you and me. Suffering and testing are inevitable in the life of a Christian.

The Promise of the Lions' Den

Daniel was not kept from the lions, but he was kept in the midst of them. God has not promised to keep us from difficulty, but He has promised to keep us in the midst of it.

When I first began to travel, I had a very difficult time with it. I was afraid something would happen to me and I'd never see my family again. But one day I read this statement: "A man of God in the will of God is immortal until his work on earth is done." I don't worry anymore, because if I'm in the will of God, going where God wants me to go, I'm all right. When God is done with me, I don't want to be around here anymore.

The Purpose of the Lions' Den

If God is a good God and in control, why would He ever let any of His children go through the kind of testing described in Daniel? God took the lions' den and used it for His glory and purpose. After the lions' den incident, King Darius made a decree that "In every dominion of my kingdom men must tremble and fear before the God of Daniel. For He is the living God, and steadfast forever; His kingdom is the one which shall not be destroyed, and His dominion shall endure to the end. He delivers and rescues, and He works signs and wonders in heaven and on earth, who has delivered Daniel from the power of the lions" (Daniel 6:26-27). At the beginning of the chapter we have a new regime. At the end of the chapter we have a new religion, by the decree of the king who was touched by the power of the almighty God.

The Prosperity of the Lions' Den

The glory of God was the first purpose of the difficulties; the prosperity of Daniel was the second. Daniel prospered. The purpose of testing is to glorify God, but it is also to purify us. Whenever we are purified, we prosper. Whenever God puts us in the furnace and drains off all the dross, we come out as pure gold.

We may not be asked to face a den of lions, but God is asking us to live our lives honestly before a watching world, unashamed to give testimony to our faith in Jesus Christ.

APPLICATION

1. The eleventh chapter of Hebrews chronicles what happens in the life of one who believes in God. Read the following verses and list the people and what they did by faith:

Hebrews 11:4-5

Hebrews 11:7-8

Hebrews 11:11

Hebrews 11:22-23

Hebrews 11:32-33

What people and events could you add to the list that are more contemporary?

2. Read the following examples of what happens to some who try to harm God's anointed:

Esther 3:1-6; 7:1-10

Psalm 7:14-16

Daniel 6:3-5, 11-13, 24

Acts 12:1-23

What seems to be the motivation for these people's actions?

3. Daniel faced the lions because he was persistent in his faith. Are there any ravenous beasts who are after you? If your answer is yes, what are they?

What could Daniel have done to avoid the lions? What would he have missed had he done so?

What is your response to the lions you face?

Read 1 Peter 5:8-9.

4. Read Psalm 34:7 and 97:10. God hasn't promised we will never face difficulty. What has He promised?

What difficulties have you faced in your life?

How has God kept you in the midst of them?

5. Read Daniel 6:20-27. What percentage of this passage is about God?

How does the story of Daniel and the lions' den glorify God?

Have you seen God glorified in your own difficulties?

Have you known anyone who was drawn to God because of their difficulties or someone else's difficulties? If so, how did this come about?

6. Read the following verses:

Job 23:10

Daniel 6:28

James 1:12

How do you think we become purified through testing?

Look back on a time when you endured temptation and stood fast. What was the result in your own life? What, if any, were the effects on people around you?

7. John Bunyan, kept in prison because he would not agree to stop preaching, wrote, "Unless I am willing to pluck out my eyes and let the blind lead me, then God Almighty being my witness and my defense—if it shall please Him to let frail life last that long— the moss shall grow on my eyebrows before I surrender my principles or violate my conscience."

How firm do you hold to your principles and your faith?

DID YOU KNOW?

A historian named Montgomery cites an incident in the reign of Darius III in 336 to 331 B.C. Darius III put to death a man he knew was innocent. Immediately Darius repented and blamed himself for having greatly erred. But it was not possible to undo what was done because the laws of the Medes and Persians were unalterable. The Persian kings were considered infallible—therefore, anything they said was irreversible.

God's Animal Parade

Daniel 7:1-8

In this lesson we will begin looking at the first vision of Daniel.

OUTLINE

As we study Daniel's first dream, we will see how God's viewpoint of history differed from Nebuchadnezzar's viewpoint of the future.

  I. **The Setting of Daniel's Dream**
 II. **The Sequence of Daniel's Dream**
 A. The First Beast
 B. The Second Beast
 C. The Third Beast
 D. The Fourth Beast
 E. The Fifth Kingdom
III. **The Schooling of Daniel's Dream**
 A. The Progress of Human History
 B. The Preservation of Human History
 C. The Purpose of Human History

OVERVIEW

Professor Alfred Weber, a great historian, wrote a few years ago in *Farewell to European History*, "To the one endowed with historical perspective, it must be clear that we are in the end of world history as we know it."

No matter how one reads history or ponders the prophecies of secular or religious prophets, we all recognize that strange things are happening in the world today. Unrest is almost everywhere in our world. It feels like war could break out at any time in four or five key spots around the globe. Self-destruction does not seem unlikely. What will be the final outcome of the nations in this period of history? Can anyone know? Yes, we can know. We cannot know all the details, but God has provided for us a broad scope of prophecy.

According to Dr. John Walvoord, former President of Dallas Theological Seminary, the seventh chapter of Daniel "provides the most comprehensive and detailed prophecy of future events that you will find anywhere in the Old Testament." But it is not a linear book. The message is not consecutive. The first six chapters of Daniel are an historic chronology. Chapters seven through twelve are visions that took place during the period historically described in chapters one through six.

Daniel's four dreams took place over a period of twenty-two years. In Daniel 1 through 6, Daniel interpreted dreams for others. In chapters seven through twelve, Daniel interpreted his own dreams. Chapter two is a dream given to Nebuchadnezzar and interpreted by Daniel. Chapter seven is a dream given to Daniel and interpreted by an angel. Chapter two relates Nebuchadnezzar's viewpoint of history, the great accomplishment of humanity. Chapter seven gives God's viewpoint of that same time—a bunch of ravenous beasts devouring one another.

The Setting of Daniel's Dream

Daniel is the first apocalyptic writer in the Bible. He wrote and conveyed prophetic truth by means of signs and symbols. He had a vision, and the symbols of his dream were threefold.

First of all, he saw a great sea. Four seas are generally mentioned in the Bible: the Galilean Sea, the Red Sea, the Dead Sea, and the Great Sea. The Great Sea was the Mediterranean. In his dream, Daniel was standing by the great Mediterranean Sea.

But there is also a figurative meaning to the word "sea." That is the great "sea of humanity."

The second thing Daniel saw in his dream was four winds blowing on that sea. The number four in the Bible often stands for the earth. We have the four winds from the four corners of the world, the four points of the compass, and the four seasons. In this passage, Daniel is picturing a gigantic sea with winds from all of the four points of the compass blowing in upon that sea. It is a picture of the world's condition. The striving of the wind upon the sea denotes political strife and uprisings, wars and bloodshed among the nations.

The third thing Daniel saw was four great beasts coming out of the sea. In the ancient world, generally speaking, animals were used as symbols of kingdoms even as they are today. Today the lion represents Great Britain. The eagle represents the United States. Almost every nation has its own animal representative. These beasts coming up out of the sea were kingdoms that have existed in the world.

The Sequence of Daniel's Dream

The words of sequence in verses four through eight are very important. The beasts didn't all come up at the same time. They followed each other, one at a time. Each of these beasts represents a chronology of kingdoms exactly as in Daniel 2. The first, the head of gold, was Babylon. The second, the arms and the chest of silver, was Medo-Persia. The third, the belly of bronze, was Greece. And the fourth, the legs of iron, was Rome. The interpretation of chapter seven will be of the same nations in the same sequence, only we will see it from God's viewpoint. As God looks at them, they are bestial—they are animals.

The First Beast

The first beast was like a lion that had eagle wings. The lion is the king of beasts and the eagle is the king of birds. This animal symbolizes the Babylonian empire which in Daniel 2 was symbolized by the head of gold. The head of gold has now become a lion in God's eyes.

The national symbol of Babylon was a winged lion. The wings indicate the swift conquest of a strong and cruel kingdom. This first beast combines the majesty of the lion and the strength and power of an eagle. In Jeremiah 49:19-22, the eagle and the lion are both used to describe Nebuchadnezzar. Daniel is very specific when he gives prophecies.

Daniel 7:4 says of the winged lion, "I watched till its wings were plucked off; and it was lifted up from the earth and made to stand on two feet like a man, and a man's heart was given to it." When Nebuchadnezzar was proud of his Babylonian Empire, God struck him down and he became a beast. He walked on all fours and ate grass. That's kind of like being plucked.

Like Nebuchadnezzar at his return of sanity, the beast got up on two feet. The beast was even given a heart like a man. The beast out of the sea is the Babylonian Empire.

The Second Beast

The second animal is a bear. Babylon fell to Medo-Persia. In keeping with the sequence in Daniel two, the next kingdom is Medo-Persia.

There are thirteen references to bears in the Bible. Every time they are mentioned, they are cast in a context of ferocious, violent behavior. These bears have appetites that are never satisfied. This second kingdom was never satisfied until she reached from the Indus River on the east to the land of Egypt and the Aegean Sea on the west. God granted this second kingdom the authority to subjugate many nations like a greedy bear.

In the dream, there were three ribs in the mouth of the bear. Historians tell us that Medo-Persia conquered Lydia, Babylon, and Egypt. The ribs in the mouth of the bear were the victims of the previous hunt. Still the bear was not satisfied.

Daniel also saw that the bear was lifted up on one side. I picture a circus bear doing a trick with two paws on one side held up. What was the meaning? In the Medo-Persian Empire, the Persians were dominant. By the end of the Book of Daniel, the Medes were about gone. The Persians were in control.

The Third Beast

"After this I looked, and there was another, like a leopard, which had on its back four wings of a bird. The beast also had four heads, and dominion was given to it" (Daniel 7:6). The leopard represented Greece. It is known in the animal kingdom as swift, cunning, cruel, with an insatiable appetite for blood. This is in keeping with Daniel 2 and could be none other than the Greek Empire under Alexander the Great. History records that Persia was defeated by Greece. The four wings on the back of the leopard speak of the conquest and of its ability to strike fast.

This leopard had four heads. History tells us that after Alexander the Great died in 323 B.C., his kingdom was divided among his four generals—Ptolemy, Seleucus, Lysimachus and Cassander. This fits the picture of the four-headed leopard.

The Scripture goes on to say dominion was given to him. With 35,000 soldiers, Alexander the Great went up against the Medo-Persian army of 200,000 to 300,000 soldiers and miraculously won. Everybody said it was the military strategy of Alexander the Great. But it was God who gave the dominion to him. Alexander was subject to a higher power. God is sovereign.

The Fourth Beast

Chapter two of Daniel says about Rome, "the fouth kingdom shall be as strong as iron, inasmuch as iron breaks in pieces and shatters everything; and like iron that crushes, that kingdom will break in pieces and crush all the others" (v. 40). This is the iron kingdom of Rome.

In the seventh chapter, the beast is described as "dreadful and terrible, exceedingly strong. It had huge iron teeth; it was devouring, breaking in pieces, and trampling the residue with its feet. It was different from all the beasts that were before it, and it had ten horns" (v. 7). There isn't any animal in the animal kingdom to which we can compare the fourth beast. There wasn't anything Daniel could describe, when he saw this horrible beast representing the imperialistic and cruel materialism of Rome. Imperialistic Rome was known for her cruelty.

It was Rome that invented crucifixion. It was Rome that crucified Peter. It was Rome that beheaded Paul. It was Rome that banished John. It was Rome that burned the Christians. It was Rome that crucified our Lord. Truly it was different from all the beasts that were before it in its cruelty.

The ten horns are ten kingdoms who rule simultaneously. Among them one will appear who, conquering the others, will eventually dominate the entire empire and become the world dictator. We are talking here about the Antichrist. There has never been a ten-part Roman empire, so this has to be future. Most prophetic scholars believe this part of the prophecy will be fulfilled in some kind of a revived Roman empire, perhaps even something like the European Common Market.

The Fifth Kingdom

When we call this ten-part empire the fifth kingdom, we are not exactly accurate, because these ten horns grow out of the head of the fourth beast. They are a last development of the fourth beast. This suggests that Rome was not destroyed, nor did it disappear. Rome is the only kingdom that did not get conquered by a greater power. Rome did not die. She fell apart because of internal corruption and rottenness. The nations of Western Europe and those adjacent to the Mediterranean Sea are still a part of what was once the Roman Empire. Nations that immigrated to Rome did not found a new kingdom, but intermarried into the Roman families and continued the old Roman kingdom without dominion.

The Schooling of Daniel's Dream

I think God is trying to teach us something in this passage about the progress of human history. Evolution in human history is not observable. Modern technological progress in no way invalidates what I have just said, because it is international justice, peace, and human government that show national identity and security. These realms are hard to find as we study history in progress. Although humankind glories in the advances and achievements of civilization through the centuries, God clearly sees human history as a chronicle of immorality, brutality, and depravity. Government and its leaders may mask their true character from people for a time, but they are always unmasked before God. Just as we have moved from the royal lion to the beast, as human history unfolds it does not get better, it gets worse.

Another lesson is the preservation of human history. All of the secular prophets are prophesying that we won't last as a civilization much past the year 2000. God says that won't happen. While the civilization of the ten kingdoms is still intact, Jesus will come back. So the world will remain when Christ comes back.

The third lesson has to do with the purpose of human history. Why would God allow the kingdoms to get worse and worse, destroying and devouring each other? I think it is because God is giving humanity an opportunity to demonstrate how inept they are at trying to rule the world God created. All of the coups, plots, rebellions, all of the chaos is just a reminder that what man has never been able to do, God in heaven has in control. And one day King Jesus is going to come and set it right.

APPLICATION

1. Daniel is not a book like other books in the Bible. It does not follow consecutively in its message. Compare the following verses, noting their order:

Daniel 5:30 and Daniel 7:1; 8:1

Daniel 5:31 and Daniel 9:1-2

Daniel 6:28 and Daniel 10:1

Chapters one through seven of Daniel reveal the destinies of the nations of the world. Chapters eight through twelve reveal the destiny of the nation of Israel. After the seventh chapter, there is no more Aramaic language written in the story. Why do you think that happens?

2. Often in the Bible, the word "sea" is used for great masses and multitudes of people. Read the following verses:

Isaiah 17:12-13

Isaiah 57:20

Revelation 17:15

What are the different words used to describe the people symbolized in these verses?

What do you think the Great Sea in Daniel 7:2-3 is symbolizing?

3. Read the following verses about wind and its relation to the sea:

Jeremiah 25:32

Daniel 7:2

Luke 21:25

Revelation 7:1

4. In the Bible, animals are often used to represent kingdoms. Read the following passages and list the kingdoms and their representative animals:

Psalm 74:13-14

Jeremiah 4:7

Jeremiah 49:19-22

Ezekiel 29:3-5

Ezekiel 32:2

Daniel 7:3-7

5. The second kingdom, Medo-Persia, is symbolized as a bear. According to the following verses, how are bears portrayed in the Bible?

1 Samuel 17:34-37

2 Samuel 17:8

2 Kings 2:23-24

Proverbs 17:12

Hosea 13:8

6. Why do you think God allows terrible kingdoms, one after another, to succeed each other? What do you think might be His purpose in that?

Read Isaiah 64:1-2. What do you think Isaiah was frustrated about?

Read Revelation 19:11. How will God finally answer the chaos?

Greece was the progenitor of the military strategy we call the blitzkrieg. They are the ones who started the strategy of striking fast, striking quick, making it happen. Alexander the Great conquered most of the civilized world, all the way from Macedonia to Africa and eastward to India. The lightning character of his conquest is without precedent in the ancient world.

Ancient of Days

Daniel 7:9-14

In this lesson we will learn about Daniel's prophecy concerning the kingdom of God versus the kingdoms of humanity.

OUTLINE

A s we study this prophecy, we will examine what will happen in the throne room of God and what simultaneously will happen on earth. We will also look at Daniel's description of God and the Kingdom of Jesus Christ.

I. **The Ancient of Days in Heaven**
   A. His Eternity
   B. His Purity
   C. His Majesty
   D. His Authority
   E. His Deity
II. **The Beast on Earth**
III. **The Son of Man in Heaven**
IV. **The Kingdom of Jesus Christ**
   A. Unlimited
   B. Unique
   C. Unified
   D. Universal
   E. Unending
   F. Unconquerable

OVERVIEW

D avid L. Cooper, in his studies on the Book of Daniel, wrote that in order to understand Daniel's dream, you have to dream yourself. You need to imagine you are watching Daniel's vision on a motion picture screen. And the screen is split. There is a top section and a bottom section. The film begins in the first part of chapter seven in the lower half of the screen, showing the beasts coming up out of the water, one at a time. When the terrible fourth beast is devouring the nations, the picture on the upper level suddenly comes alive. We see the Ancient of Days seated in the throne room of glory in heaven. On that divided screen, we see what is happening in heaven while we view the last gasp of the Roman Empire on earth.

One of the problems in studying and interpreting prophecy is that as the Old Testament prophets looked at the future, often it converged together for them. It would be like driving toward a mountain range and thinking there was one gigantic peak ahead of you. But when you get closer you realize there is a great valley between two peaks. Daniel, Isaiah, and Jeremiah looked to the future and saw the coming of Jesus Christ. They saw Him as coming to be born and coming to reign. But they did not know those would be two separate events, separated by many years.

An example of this is seen in Isaiah 61:1-2. "The Spirit of the Lord God is upon Me, because the Lord has anointed Me to preach good tidings to the poor; He has sent Me to heal the brokenhearted, to proclaim liberty to the captives, and the opening of the prison to those who are bound; to proclaim the acceptable year of the Lord, and the day of vengeance of our God." This is a prophecy concerning the first coming of Jesus to the earth. It lists the things Jesus would do when He came. But it adds, "the day of vengeance of our God"—a happening that is associated with His second coming. When Jesus read this passage in the synagogue to describe His earthly ministry at the time, He stopped before the line about vengeance, even though it was part of the sentence. He closed the book. Because that part of the prophecy would not happen for at least nineteen hundred years.

In Daniel 7, this same type of thing happens. Daniel was speaking about ancient kingdoms, then he mentioned the ten horns of the Roman Empire. That takes us to the time when the Lord will come again. All in this passage about the king and the Antichrist and the Son of man is removed from Daniel 7:7 by over two thousand years.

The Ancient of Days in Heaven

This chapter is the only chapter in the Bible where the Ancient of Days is mentioned. It is mentioned here three times. It is the only passage in the Bible that pictures God in human form. He is not human. He is Spirit. But Daniel visualizes God as we would see God if we could understand what God would look like. He sees God the Father as the Ancient of Days. The term literally means, "the elderly One," "the One who has been around forever," "the One who never had a beginning." As he looks at God, he sees Him in His holiness, eternity and glory. Almost all of the major attributes of God the Father are pictured in the scene that Daniel sees when he looks into heaven.

Here is the contrast. The bottom of the screen is turmoil, upheaval, chaos, beasts and terrible things. The top half of the screen is the majestic throne room of glory, with the Ancient of Days seated upon the throne.

The Bible describes Him first of all in His eternity. He is the Ancient of Days. He is the Source of time. He never had a beginning. He was never born. He was forever and forever.

Next Daniel said, "His garment was white as snow" (Daniel 7:9). Whenever we see the term "white as snow" in the Bible, it is a picture of absolute purity. Daniel sees God the Father seated on His throne in absolute purity.

He also sees God in His majesty. God is seated on a throne, a throne that has been "put in place" (v. 9). It was put into position. God is the Sovereign Judge of the universe. He is about to judge the world.

Next, we see Him in His authority. Daniel says, "His throne was a fiery flame, its wheels a burning fire" (v. 9). Many commentators believe the image of the fiery wheels pictures the possibility that the throne could go anywhere in the universe to bring judgment.

"A fiery stream issued and came forth from before Him" (v. 10). This is again a picture of the judgment of God. In all of the Bible we are continually exposed to fire as a preparation for the judging God. It depicts God's presence.

Finally in Daniel's vision, we see God's deity. "A thousand thousands ministered to Him; ten thousand times ten thousand stood before Him" (v. 10). This is not necessarily meant to be taken literally. It is a reminder to us of the tremendous number of angelic bodies that are before Him, bowing down and worshipping Him. He alone is worthy to be worshipped.

Then Daniel says, "And the books were opened" (v. 10). The judgment is about to begin. The written evidence is produced. God is about to judge the beastly nations of the world. The books are opened, and God is going to read the activity of the nations. He will read about their blasphemy and their idolatry and judge them guilty.

One commentator has written that in spite of all the different interpretations of this chapter, the chapter claims unambiguously that the Most High is reigning in heaven. His enemies think He is not in control, but He is in control all the same. He is the sovereign God who rules and reigns. On the bottom half of the split screen, there is turmoil on earth. On the top half, the Ancient of Days is seated in the throne room of glory, opening the books. He is in control.

The Beast on Earth

Moving to Daniel 7:11-12, we are drawn back to the bottom half of the screen. Verses eleven and twelve tell us in rapid-fire description that the Beast was slain. Who is the Beast? The Beast is the Antichrist. He has risen up as a part of the fourth dynasty, his body is consumed in the fire, and the dramatic turn of events that takes place now is a picture of the sovereignty of our Divine Judge. The Beast will reign over the earth for three and a half years and then he will be destroyed by the Supreme Judge of the whole world. Then he will be cast into the Lake of Fire.

Satan is not cast into the Lake of Fire until later. The first two to be thrown in are the Beast and the False Prophet (see Revelation 19:20). They are thrown in as God from heaven judges them guilty of sin and rebellion. The reign of terror of the Antichrist and the persecution of God's saints on earth has run its course. The Antichrist's cup of iniquity is full. Christ, whose name he has blasphemed and whose followers he has killed, consigns the Antichrist to the Lake of Fire, his final and proper doom.

The Son of Man in Heaven

In verse 13, we are finished with the events on earth and we are back in heaven again. Daniel says, "I was watching in the night visions, and behold, One like the Son of Man, coming with the clouds of heaven! He came to the Ancient of Days, and they brought Him near before Him" (v. 13). We see the Son of Man in His human form. He has been given the privilege of judging the world. God the Father gave Him "dominion and glory and a kingdom, that all peoples, nations, and languages should serve Him. His dominion is an everlasting dominion, which shall not pass away, and His kingdom the one which shall not be destroyed" (v. 14). And He shall reign forever and forever.

The Kingdom of Jesus Christ

The kingdom of Jesus Christ superceded everything that happened on the bottom half of the screen, the kingdoms of humanity. In every way it was better. In every way it was greater.

Unlimited

In Daniel's description of the kingdom of Christ, we find that it is unlimited. The kingdom of this world is throttled. Jesus Christ will be given dominion, all dominion without limitation. He will be the absolute monarch of the whole world.

Unique

We also find that the kingdom of Jesus Christ is unique, while the kingdoms of this world are typical. The Bible says there was given to Him dominion and glory. That's the difference in the kingdom of Jesus Christ. It's not a kingdom for its own sake. It is a kingdom for the glory of God. It's a kingdom filled with deity, a glorious kingdom. We have never seen anything like what God has in store when He sets up His kingdom.

Unified

His kingdom is unified, while the kingdoms of this world are torn. The chaos and disruption and upheaval in the governments we see in Daniel didn't stop with the Roman Empire. It is going on today. In our world, human government is described by chaos, but when Christ comes back He will rule a kingdom.

Universal

The kingdom of Jesus Christ is universal. The kingdoms of this world are territorial. The Bible says that His kingdom is over all people, and all nations, and all languages, and all of them are going to serve Him. Even the greatest kingdoms of Babylon and Rome and Greece, which were considered by historians to be worldwide kingdoms, did not cover all of the territory. But when Jesus comes to set up His kingdom, it is going to stretch from east to west to north to south. It will cover every little corner of the globe and there will be no place where you can avoid the kingdom of God. Christ rules universally throughout the whole world.

Unending

The kingdom of our Lord is unending, while the kingdoms of this world are temporary. The Scripture says His dominion is ever-lasting, and it shall not pass away. Every king who came to authority thought he would reign forever, or his descendants after him. Yet we have discovered that even the great Babylon, which seemed impregnable with its 387 feet high walls and its eighty-seven foot thickness, one day fell. There was not a kingdom that ever survived like the kingdom of Jesus Christ—unending, forever and forever.

Unconquerable

Finally, the kingdom of Jesus Christ is unconquerable, while the kingdoms of this world are triumphed over by each other. The Scripture says His kingdom shall not be destroyed. Who would destroy it? Who rivals King Jesus? Who can come and make a threat against the kingdom of our Lord and our God? There isn't anyone. It will never be destroyed.

What Daniel is trying to teach us is that what seems to be great-ness in the kingdom of humans is nothing when compared with the greatness of the kingdom of Jesus Christ. When we see what God has in store for those who love Him, it helps to understand what's going on in our world without getting too upset.

When we are Christians, there is a glad excitement for what will come when we have already experienced in some small way the kingdom of Christ in our hearts. Jesus took the fear out of what will happen at the judgment by what He did on the cross. He made it possible for everyone to be an expectant anticipator of the coming of Christ, if they will just put Him where He belongs—on the throne in their hearts.

APPLICATION

1. God the Father is the Ancient of Days, the Source of time. Read the following verses:

Psalm 29:10

Psalm 90:2

Isaiah 57:15

What is the closest you can come to understanding the concept of Someone who always was?

Meditating on this, does it change your perception of God at all? If so, in what way?

2. Read the following verses. What attributes of God are they showing?

Psalm 50:3

Psalm 51:7

Psalm 93:1-2

Psalm 97:3

Can you think of some other symbols that are used to portray characteristics of God? If so, what are they and what do they portray?

3. What are some of the books God has in His library? Read the following verses:

Exodus 32:32

Psalm 56:8

Malachi 3:16

Revelation 20:12

What things are recorded in the books?

What do you think is written about you in the books that God has?

4. In Daniel 7:13-14, Jesus Christ is brought before God the Father, the Ancient of Days. He stands before the throne, and God the Father gives Him the nations of the world. How do the following verses relate to this event?

Psalm 2:8

Psalm 72:11

Revelation 11:15

Revelation 19:15-16

5. The kingdom of Christ is unlimited. Below, make a list of ways worldly kingdoms and governments are limited. Then note how Christ's kingdom is not limited in any of these ways.

Worldly Kingdoms   Christ's Kingdom

6. What is your reaction when you think about the second coming of Christ?

Why do you think you have that reaction?

Is it a reaction you are happy with?

DID YOU KNOW?

One of the names of Jesus Christ often used in prophetic passages is the reference to the Son of Man. The Son of God speaks of His deity. The Son of David speaks of His royalty. The Son of Man speaks of His humanity.

The Antichrist

Daniel 7:15-28

In this lesson we will learn what the Antichrist will be like.

OUTLINE

As we study the Antichrist, we will examine his historical role and biblical characteristics. We will also see what our perspective should be on this subject.

OVERVIEW

One of the most popular indoor sports of theologians is trying to identify the Antichrist spoken of by Daniel and John. Everyone and everything from individual Roman rulers to the whole Catholic system, from the pope to Oliver Cromwell, from Hitler to John F. Kennedy, from Henry Kissinger to Judas Iscariot have been made candidates for the Antichrist.

In Revelation 13:18, we are told the number of the Antichrist is 666. People have tried to figure out who the Antichrist is by playing number games. The fun thing is that anyone can be the Antichrist if you do it right. You only have to follow three simple rules. One, if the proper name doesn't work, add a title. Two, if it doesn't work in English, try Hebrew, Greek, or Latin. Three, if none of those things work, cheat on the spelling.

Nobody knows what the number means. We won't know what it means until God wants us to know. We don't know who the Antichrist is, but we can know what he is. The Bible says he is more than just an insignificant person who will appear sometime in the future. There is a lot of information about him in the Bible. The seventh chapter of Daniel sets the stage for our understanding of the prophetic phenomena. It reminds us that the sovereign God is in control, and He takes us through the steps of human government. From the time of Daniel the prophet and the Babylonian kingdom to the end of human government when Christ the King returns, God gives us the whole scheme of things. Into that scheme, this individual fits.

In the seventh chapter of Daniel, there are signposts that help you see the epics. These are the phrases used when Daniel says he saw a vision by night, or a night vision. There are three of these. The first begins Daniel's presentation of three great kingdoms of the world (see v. 2). The second begins Daniel's vision of the fourth kingdom over which Christ will be victorious (see v. 7). The third introduces the final chapter when Christ comes to reign on earth (see v. 13).

The Antichrist fits into the last part of that second epic. At the end of the final form of the final kingdom, the Bible says a man will arise to take leadership over it. That is the Antichrist.

The Antichrist Will Be a Charismatic Leader

The world is ripe for a leader who will come upon the stage of our world scene and command the respect and following of the world, because nobody seems to have the answer to our international problems. All the world is looking for someone to solve them. When the Antichrist comes and by supernatural revelation begins to demonstrate that he has the ability to lead the world, they will be so anxious to see him come, they will fall down at his feet. The vacuum has been created.

People will be hungry for someone to follow. The Antichrist will be that type of person. He will be a charismatic leader. I don't mean he will be a Pentecostal. He will be a man with great charisma.

He will be a great public speaker. Daniel 7:8 says he has "a mouth speaking pompous words." Verse twenty echoes that, and verse twenty-five says, "He shall speak pompous words against the Most High." Later on, when the Antichrist establishes a great image everyone is supposed to worship, even the image will speak. Some think he will do it through ventriloquism; some think it will be demon possession. I don't know how he will do it, but this man will have great oratorical power.

Some have said the Antichrist will be noted for wonderful eloquence. He will be able to capture the attention and admiration of the world. He will be able to move the masses. Some have said he will be like Melanchthon, William Jennings Bryant, and Gladstone, all wrapped up in one. Everyone who hears him speak will be caught up in his charisma as a great speaker. He will be able to weld these masses into activity, and the people will follow him.

The Bible also says there will be something about him that is attractive. It says of him, his "appearance was greater than his fellows" (Daniel 7:20). The word used here means, "abundant in size, in rank." Sometimes in the Bible it has to do with being a captain or chief or lord. It is a man of high rank or impressive appearance, like Saul in the Old Testament, who was head and shoulders above his fellows. This man, when he walks into the presence of others, will immediately capture their attention. Something about his very person will attract people, by an inhuman magnetism, to follow him.

The Antichrist Will Be a Clever Leader

This man will be the master politician of all history, the greatest diplomat who ever lived. Verse twenty says he has eyes. That phrase has reference to his mental ability, his intellect, and his cleverness. He will be able to solve the problems of the world with his cleverness and wisdom. This is illustrated in verse eight. It says he will rise up at the time of the ten-king confederation and subdue three other kings. It describes it graphically, saying the three horns were "plucked out by the roots." This phrase means literally "to squeeze out, to push out by subterfuge, to come in and cleverly replace."

In Daniel 11:21 is another illustration of his cleverness. "And in his place shall arise a vile person, to whom they will not give the honor of royalty; but he shall come in peaceably, and seize the kingdom by intrigue." The Antichrist will be the master of malarkey. He'll be able to talk people into anything.

The Antichrist Will Be a Cultic Leader

The Antichrist will not just be in the political realm, he will also be in the realm of religion. He is a cultic leader. Daniel 7:25 says about him, "He shall speak pompous words against the Most High, shall persecute the saints of the Most High, and shall intend to change times and law." The Bible says he will stand up with his oratory and give great speeches against the Most High God.

Then he will put himself in God's place. He will ask people to fall down and worship him. One of the people later on in the Book of Daniel is a historical type of the Antichrist. His name was Antiochus Epiphanes IV. He illustrates this concept in the Antichrist of self-worship. On the coins that survive from that day can be seen the figure of Zeus, whose features closely resemble those of Antiochus Epiphanes. One of those coins, which is now in the British Museum, has this inscription on it: "King Antiochus, God Manifest, Victory Bearer."

In his cultic leadership, the Antichrist will try to change the moral and natural laws of the universe. Verse twenty-five says he "shall intend to change times." Most people believe that means he will mess around with the calendar. He will do away with religious feast days. Some think he may try to get rid of the seven-day week, which is God-ordained time, and change it to a ten-day week like they tried to do during the French Revolution. He will try to strip down everything that has anything to do with structure, anything that has to do with history and stability as far as religious beliefs are concerned. He'll take it away and start over from scratch. He will start his own religion to obliterate God from the picture.

The Bible says he shall intend to change the law. He will create his own morality. He'll say, "You don't have to follow the morality of God. Here is a new set of laws."

He will also be able to do great things. How could a man like him be able to get enough people to follow him so he could rule the world? Second Thessalonians 2:9 tells us he will be equipped by Satan to do great wonders and great lies and great signs. He will heal. I believe he'll bring people back from the grave—at least give the appearance of it. He will be able to do things this world hasn't seen done since Jesus walked on the earth.

The Antichrist Will Be a Cruel Leader

The fourth beast "shall devour the whole earth, trample it and break it in pieces" (Daniel 7:23). He "shall persecute the saints of the Most High" (v. 25). Literally, he will wear them out. The people who are saved during the Tribulation period will become the targets of this man. He determines to destroy them. The believers' lives will be difficult, particularly after the Antichrist comes into full power during the last half of the Tribulation. He will harass and afflict and persecute them without mercy. Many of them will be martyred for their faith.

The phrase "to wear out the saints" is a phrase that comes out of the context of wearing out garments. It's not that he will come and just snuff them out. He will wear them out like you wear out clothes. He will harass them every minute and he won't let them breathe.

He will probably wear them out through public seizure and through economic squeeze. We know about the mark on the head and on the hand. He'll starve some of them out. Antiochus Epiphanes, the first person recorded in history to persecute a people exclusively for their religious faith, caught a group of Jews in a cave observing the Sabbath. He had the mouth of the cave sealed and fires set inside to suffocate them. That's just one example of antichrist behavior.

The Antichrist and Us

The stage is already being set for the coming of the Antichrist. How? The abject conditions of the economy in Germany after World War I helped to catapult Adolph Hitler into power. The German treasury was low in gold. The budget was unbalanced. Sound familiar? Inflation went out of perspective. In 1919 the German mark was worth twenty-five cents. Within four years, it declined in value until four trillion were needed to equal one dollar in buying power. The German middle class lost all their savings. The value of every pension was wiped out. All security was gone. The people were ready to listen to any demi-god who would help them solve their bitterness. Enter Hitler.

It was Lenin who said, "The surest way to overthrow an existing social order is to debauch the currency." What do you think would happen in the United States if a charismatic wonder-working leader were to walk across the American scene and say to us, "I have the answer to the economic stress of this country"? The stage is being set for the arrival of a man like the man we've been talking about.

The strategy of the Christian is not to look for the Antichrist. No place in the Bible does it say your job as a Christian is to look for the Antichrist. But we are to look for Christ appearing again. When we see things that signal He will be appearing soon, our attention should refocus on the One who is coming—Jesus Christ, the coming King and Savior of all humanity. The Antichrist might be alive today, but speculation about him doesn't fit either of the two things God has told us we are to do in light of the coming of Christ. Those two things are to work and to watch.

Another thing that puts this in perspective is the Bible's statement that Antichrist is already here. In the Book of 1 John we are told, "Every spirit that does not confess that Jesus Christ has come in the flesh is not of God. And this is the spirit of the Antichrist, which you have heard was coming, and is now already in the world" (1 John 4:3). The spirit of Antichrist is everywhere in the world today.

What should we do? Be aware. And know that God has all of this in control. He has a plan that includes us, but not together with the Antichrist. Someday soon we are going to hear the shout, the trumpet will sound, and we are going to be caught up to meet Jesus Christ.

APPLICATION

1. The Antichrist is known by a lot of names in the Bible. Even in the Book of Daniel, there are several names for him. Read the following verses and list the names and/or descriptions of the Antichrist:

Daniel 7:8

Daniel 8:23

Daniel 9:26

Daniel 11:3

Matthew 24:15

1 John 2:18

Revelation 13:11, 18

2. Read Daniel 7:8 again. The word "horn" stands for power and authority. Why do you think he is called a little horn?

How do you think he goes from being insignificant to being a great, gigantic king?

What people do you know who are examples of going from someone insignificant to someone famous? How is it usually accomplished?

What types of people seek fame and power?

3. Read 2 Thessalonians 2:4. What is the Antichrist trying to do?

According to Revelation 13:8, what happens to the Antichrist?

What is God's first commandment from the Ten Commandments?
See Deuteronomy 5:6-10.

Other than bowing down to the Antichrist, what are other ways that
we put "gods" before God? What are you most likely to put before
God?

4. Compare Daniel 7:7, 11, 19-25 to Revelation 13:1-10. List the
similarities in the two chapters.

5. Read Luke 19:13 and Matthew 25:13. What two things are we to do while waiting for Jesus to come again?

How do you personally achieve those things?

Read Titus 2:11-13. How are we to live as we wait? Make a list of these things mentioned in the Scripture, then grade yourself on them.

How We Are to Live   Grade

6. Read 1 John 2:18-19. Who do you think are the antichrists in our time? What makes you think these people have the spirit of the Antichrist?

What characteristics do they have? What are their practices?

What is the difference between these antichrists and the coming Antichrist?

How does the Antichrist concern you?

DID YOU KNOW?

Gematria is the science of equating a person's name with numbers, as in trying to figure out the meaning of the number 666 for the Antichrist. This science began before the "Who is the Antichrist?" debate.

The Reign of Terror

Daniel 7:15-28

In this lesson we will learn about the program and profile of the Antichrist.

OUTLINE

As we study the fourth beast, we will see where he came from and how he made his impression. We will also see his end.

I. **The Appearance of the Antichrist**
   A. Inconspicuous Beginning
      1. Politically
      2. Nationally
      3. Spiritually
      4. Providentially
   B. Intimidating Bearing
II. **Acclaim of the Antichrist**
   A. Cause of His Acclaim
   B. Character of His Acclaim
III. **The Authority of the Antichrist**

OVERVIEW

Why study prophecy? If you are committed to the exposition of Scripture, you don't really have a choice. The Bible is one-fifth prophecy. Of the one-fifth that is prophetic, one third concerns the second coming of Jesus Christ and the events that surround the Second Coming.

Next to faith, there is no subject in the Bible that is discussed more than the second coming of Jesus Christ. For every time His first coming is mentioned, His second coming is mentioned eight times. For every time the subject of atonement is mentioned, the second coming is mentioned twice. The Lord Himself refers to His coming again twenty-one times in His own words. And over fifty times in the New Testament we are told to be ready for the coming again of the Lord Jesus Christ.

In the Old Testament, the Book of Daniel is the key to understanding the Scriptures. In the New Testament, the Book of Revelation is the key to understanding the Scriptures. Daniel prefigures Revelation, and Revelation interprets Daniel. The two taken together outline the scheme of events for the future, which when studied gives any Bible student a map to chart the course of events for our day.

The Appearance of the Antichrist

First of all, note his inconspicuous beginning. Daniel 7:8 speaks of ten horns that grow up as a part of the final form of the Roman Empire. Those ten horns remind us of the ten-kingdom confederation that will be a part of the final form of the Roman Empire, which will reign upon the earth in the end times. In the ten-horn prophecy, there is a reference to an eleventh horn, a "little horn." It is an inconspicuous kingdom or king in light of the other great kings. That little horn is a reference to the Antichrist. He is the one who is insignificant in his beginning, but who grows to be the king of the earth.

In Revelation 13:1, we read that this first beast with seven heads and ten horns and ten crowns upon his heads and the name of blasphemy written on him comes up out of the sea. The word "sea" in prophetic Scripture is always a reference to masses of people. This reference means that the Antichrist rises out of multitudes of people of his day. He is not brought dramatically before the world and announced, but he inconspicuously begins his ministry behind the scenes before he is finally brought out to center stage.

We can learn something from Revelation 13 in a number of categories. First of all, politically. The Scripture says the Antichrist is out of the sea. Not only does the sea signify the great masses of people, but it is a reference to the turmoil that will reign in the end time. Isaiah the prophet speaks of the wicked, saying, "But the wicked are like the troubled sea, when it cannot rest, whose waters cast up mire and dirt" (Isaiah 57:20). The Bible says in the end times there will be wars and rumors of wars. There will be chaos reigning. There will be turmoil politically. There will be lack of any organization or political direction. Out of that turmoil will arise this leader.

As we study the personality of the Antichrist, we often run into people who want to consign him to a Jewish heritage. They say he must be a Jew because he makes a covenant with the Jewish people. That covenant indicates they consider him to be the Messiah, and no Jew would ever consider a non-Jew to be the Messiah. But the Bible does not teach that the league of the Antichrist with the Jewish nation is based on their idea that he is the Messiah. It is simply a political maneuver on his part to gain control over Israel, the center of military power.

The Bible does say the Antichrist arises out of the fourth empire, the Roman Empire. He comes out of the great empire that is reigning in the last days.

Revelation 11:7 says, "When they finish their testimony, the Beast that ascends out of the bottomless pit will make war against them, overcome them, and kill them." The Antichrist will arise out of the abyss or pit. He is nothing more than Satan incarnate. He is a demon with a body. He is Satan walking around in the flesh. Satan has always been the great imitator. Just as God was incarnated in Jesus Christ and was God embodied, so Satan will determine to do the very same thing. He will embody himself in the Antichrist.

Sometimes if you get a good picture of this evil person, it can keep you awake at night. We may wonder if at the end of time everything is going to run wild and God is going to lose control. But in Revelation 13, six different times it says that control was given to him. That is a reference not only to the fact that Satan controls the Antichrist, but it is a reference to the fact that behind it all, the sovereign hand of God is keeping it all in control. He is the One who allows it, though He does not cause it. And it never,

ever moves out of the range of His controlling hand and power. He is providentially and sovereignly in control.

The Antichrist is an intimidator by his very appearance. He is described as "a beast rising up out of the sea, having seven heads and ten horns" (Revelation 13:1). The heads are covered with the names of blasphemy. He is a terrible creature. In total appearance, the Beast was like a leopard, his feet like those of a bear, and his mouth like a lion. All three characteristics of the three previous kingdoms (see Daniel 7:4-7) are embodied in the fourth kingdom, and in its final form in the Antichrist.

The Beast of Revelation combines the features of the three previous kingdoms. Whatever the Babylonian or the Medo-Persian or the Grecian empires had of strength and brutality and swiftness will be in the final form of the world rule of the western confederation of nations—the revived Roman Empire. That final nation or kingdom will have all of the parts of the previous kingdoms embodied in the kingdom and in the king.

He will be a composite of everything that will have happened up to that time. He will be Satan's masterpiece, the best Satan can do. This Antichrist will be the epitome of Satan's desire wrapped up in one person. No wonder he is such an awful person, and such a frightening personality.

The Acclaim of the Antichrist

Revelation 13:3 says, "I saw one of his heads as if it had been mortally wounded, and his deadly wound was healed. And all the world marveled and followed the Beast." One of the heads of the Beast was wounded to death. Here again is Satan's counterfeiting activity. Jesus Christ came to the cross and died and was buried and resurrected. The resurrection power of Christ was the trust which threw the Church into growth and tremendous spiritual renewal. Satan realizes if he is going to get the acclaim of the people, he'll need to do what God did. So he will get the Beast killed—or the appearance of being killed—then bring him back to life. His resurrection will cause his great following by all of the peoples in the nations of the world, except those whose names are written in the Lamb's book. Everyone else will fall down and worship the Beast.

Several years ago there were some who thought John F. Kennedy was the Antichrist because he was killed through a wound in the head. While he was lying in state in the rotunda, there were many who thought Kennedy would revive, get up out of the coffin and become the leader of the world. That didn't happen. But think for a moment what you would have felt in your own heart and mind if you had been watching TV, seeing the endless parade before the casket, and suddenly John F. Kennedy got up, took the mike in his hand and began talking to America.

The Bible says something like this is going to happen with the Antichrist. He will receive a wound in his head. He will miraculously revive, and as a result they will follow him.

Not only that, they will worship him. Their worship will be based on two fundamental facts: his uniqueness and his great military exploits. They will be saying, "Who is like the Beast? Who is able to make war with him?" (Revelation 13:4). Nobody will be able to stand up against him. He will be conqueror wherever he goes.

The Authority of the Antichrist

Once the Antichrist has brought together three nations out of the European confederacy and gets control over them, then he will get control over the ten confederate nations. After that, realizing he needs to deal with the Jews, he will go to Israel and make a covenant with the Jewish people. The covenant will allow them to continue their worship and Temple practices. He will support them and protect them until three and a half years pass. Then he will walk into the Temple and desecrate it, taking their worship away and causing all-out war between himself and the Jews. The Bible says that during this reign he will kill the two witnesses God sent to earth. He will be responsible for slaying the 144,000 witnesses. He will corrupt the name of God and the people of God and take hold of a three-fold program that he will believe gives him absolute control in the world.

The program is first of all religious. He is a blasphemer. Secondly, it is political. He is a military man. Thirdly, it is economic. He puts the "mark" on the people, and it's their credit card. If you don't have one, you can't buy and sell. He is the absolute ruler over the economy. He's got everybody just where he wants them.

The authority of the Antichrist extends to all people—all except those who are written in the Book of Life. Everyone is under his control.

Revelation 13:9 tells us something important is going to happen now. Verse nine is an exclamation point. It says, "Attention every-body. If you miss everything else in this chapter, don't miss verse nine and what follows."

Revelation 13:9 says, "If anyone has an ear, let him hear." Then verse 10 says, "He who leads into captivity shall go into captivity; he who kills with the sword must be killed with the sword. Here is the patience and the faith of the saints."

It's saying that though the reign of the Antichrist is worldwide and his dominion without peer, his end is in sight! The Antichrist will reign for a time, but then he will be destroyed.

If you study the Book of Revelation, you can find his end right in that book. The Bible says the Antichrist and his followers will come to war with Jesus Christ and His followers, and the Lamb will overcome. Then in Revelation 19:20, you see the Beast cast into the lake of fire burning with brimstone, along with the False Prophet. When the Devil is thrown into the lake of fire, the other two are still there (see Revelation 20:10).

It's tremendous to know all about this, but it would be frighten-ing if we didn't have the last chapter. God, by the Spirit, has given us the last chapter. He says to us who read it that the Antichrist, who is the best Satan has to offer, is going to reign for a time, but it is limited. His end is in sight. The King will come and set up His eternal reign and dominion. And He shall reign forever and ever.

The thing I get so excited about when I study this prohecy is that I am on the winning side. I know all about the fight, but I know who's going to win and I have cast my lot with the King of Kings.

APPLICATION

1. Jesus refers to His second coming many times. Read the following:

Matthew 10:23

Matthew 24:26-27

Mark 13:32-37

Luke 12:35-40

Luke 21:25-28

John 14:18

John 16:21-22

What are the major points Jesus makes as He talks about His coming again? List them.

Which verse gives you the most comfort?

2. Read Revelation 11:7. Where does the Beast come from?

Read Isaiah 14:12-15. How did Satan end up in the pit?

Read Revelation 20:14. What is the end to Death and Hades?

3. Read Revelation 13:1. For the meaning of the seven heads of the Beast, read Revelation 17:9.

Many tell us that is just a picture of the Roman dominion of this Antichrist. Others tell us the seven heads are seven consecutive kings of Rome, the Antichrist being the last one. Whichever it is, what is your impression of this beast? What do you picture in your head?

4. Read the following verses. What are the different ways the writer relates that power is given to the Antichrist?

Revelation 13:2

Revelation 13:4

Revelation 13:5

Revelation 13:7

In what kind of a different light does this put the Antichrist?

Who are two who are more powerful than the Antichrist?

5. Almighty God is omnipotent—all-powerful. No one can come close to His measureless power. Read the following chapters:

Job 38

Job 39

Psalm 104

What event or part of creation or anything else demonstrates to you the most about the power of God?

How does the power of God relate to the end times?

6. Read Revelation 19:20 and 20:10. What is the good news about the story of the end times? Read Revelation 21:1-7.

DID YOU KNOW?

Dr. Criswell wrote of the Beast this way: "Think of the golden majesty of Babylon, of the mighty, ponderous massiveness of Cyrus and Persia, think of the beauty, elegance and intellect of the ancient Greek world, think of the Roman with his laws and his order and his idea of justice. All of these glories will be summed up in the majesty of this one eventual Antichrist who will be like a Nebuchadnezzar, like a Cyrus by a Tiglath-Pileser, like a Shalmaneser, like a Julius Caesar, like a Caesar Augustus, like an Alexander the Great, like a Napoleon Bonaparte, like a Frederick the Great and Charlemagne all bound up into one."

The Church and the Tribulation

Selected Scriptures from Daniel

In this lesson we will see that the pretribulational view is consistent with all passages of Scripture.

OUTLINE

A s we study the Tribulation and its relation to the Church, we will learn why the Church will not be present at the time of the Tribulation.

    I. **Definition of the Tribulation**
        A. Reasons
            1. To purge the Jewish rebels
            2. To punish the Gentile rejecters
        B. Revelation
    II. **Dependence on Consistent Interpretation**
  III. **The Discussion of the Tribulation Period**
  IV. **The Deliverance Promise**
    V. **The Doctrine of Imminency**

I n the study of prophecy, there are four different views about the Tribulation period. First there is the post-tribulational view. This view teaches that the Church will go through seven years of tribulation and when it is over, the Church will be raptured and taken home to be with the Lord.

Another view is called the mid-tribulation rapture position. This view teaches that at the end of three and a half years the Church is raptured and not here for the next three and a half years of the Tribulation.

The view I believe, according to our creeds and doctrinal statement, is the pretribulation rapture. This view teaches that before the tribulation starts, the Church will be raptured and taken away from here.

There is one other view called the partial rapture view. A man named Witness Lee teaches that only those believers who are spiritual will be raptured when the Lord comes back. The rest of the Church will have to go through the Tribulation. It's kind of a Protestant purgatory.

There isn't any evidence in the Word of God that such a thing will happen. The Bible teaches the unity of the Body. God isn't going to have part of the Body up there while the rest of the Body is down here. The Church will be caught up together to be with the Lord. Another problem with the partial rapture theory is that it says our works determine in some respect how we escape punitive judgment. That isn't consistent with the Bible.

We believe in the pretribulational rapture position simply because of what the Bible teaches us about the nature of our Christian faith. The Bible teaches that the moment a person believes in Jesus Christ, he passes out of death into life and there is no condemnation hanging over him. Those who believe in post-tribulationism believe there is condemnation hanging over them, which they will experience for seven years on this earth.

Definition of the Tribulation

The Tribulation period in the Bible is defined as the final period of Jehovah's determined dealings with Daniel's people in order to finish Israel's transgressions. There are two reasons for the Tribulation period. First of all, it is to purge out the Jewish rebels.

Second, it is to punish Gentile rejecters. The Bible teaches that during the seven year period of time, the wrath of God is going to come primarily upon the Jews, but even the Gentiles who have rejected Christ during that time will be the objects of the wrath of God.

The definition of the tribulation period is given to us in great detail in the Book of Revelation. Revelation is a self-interpreting book. It is a book that tells you what the signs are, then what those signs mean. At the beginning of the book there is an outline right in the text (see Revelation 1:19). The outline is three-fold: the things John saw, the things which were, and the things which would be thereafter.

Revelation 1:1-20 is the record of what John saw when he was on the Isle of Patmos. That is the first subject on the outline. Revelation two and three deal with the seven churches of Revelation. That is the second subject, the things which are. Beginning at chapter four to the end of Revelation is the third subject, "the things which will take place after this" (Revelation 1:19).

Beginning at Revelation four through the nineteenth chapter, almost all of the information has to do with the period we know as the Tribulation. In that section of Scripture are the vials and judgments, bowls, trumpets and seals that picture the pouring out of God's wrath on this earth. The word "church" appears nineteen times in Revelation 1-3. It is not mentioned once as being on earth in chapters 4-19. During the time of tribulation in Revelation, the Church is not mentioned one time. Why? Because the Tribulation will be going on down here on earth when the Church is up there with God. The Church will not be present at the Tribulation, so there is no reason to mention it.

Dependence on Consistent Interpretation

The doctrine of pretribulation is not dependent on one passage of Scripture, but on the consistent interpretation of all passages of Scripture where the truth is mentioned. Let's look first at 2 Thessalonians.

The believers in Thessalonica thought the Tribulation period had already started and they were living in the midst of it. Paul wrote the second letter to the Thessalonians first of all to tell them they were not in the tribulation. He also wrote to answer their question, "Was Paul right when he taught that we would not go through the Tribulation?"

Paul lists the things that must happen before the Tribulation can happen. He says first of all, "That Day will not come unless the falling away comes first" (2 Thessalonians 2:3). The phrase "falling away" is literally "apostasy." Most Bible students understand that word to mean the Tribulation period will follow hard on the heels of a time when the church at large leaves the faith. It is a time of tremendous declension within the Church.

The second thing that must happen is "the man of sin is revealed, the son of perdition" (v. 3). The Tribulation period will not come in full force until the falling away and the revelation of the man of sin, the Antichrist.

The third thing is in 2 Thessalonians 2:6-7: "And now you know what is restraining, that he may be revealed in his own time. For the mystery of lawlessness is already at work; only He who now restrains will do so until He is taken out of the way." The Tribulation period can't go into full force until the restraining influence in the world is taken out of the way. Who is the restrainer? There are a number of different ideas on this subject. Some believe it is human government. Some believe it is a particular law. Some believe it is some individual alive in the world.

But the Bible is very clear about what restrains in the life of an individual, and I personally believe this is a very clear reference to the Holy Spirit. The restrainer is the Holy Spirit. The Holy Spirit lives in us, and when we leave here, the Holy Spirit will leave with us. The only thing that holds this world together is the restraining influence of the Holy Spirit, who lives in the hearts and lives of every single believer. The day of Tribulation cannot begin until the Holy Spirit is taken out of the way. That's going to happen when the Rapture occurs.

The Discussion of the Tribulation Period

After describing the sevenfold condition of the visible Church in chapters two and three, John writes about the twenty-four elders who are in heaven (see Revelation 4:4). He says these elders are significant because they are seated, robed, and have crowns upon their heads. These significant things suggest the twenty-four are symbolic representations of the Church. Where is the Church at the outset of the Tribulation period? It is seated, clothed, and crowned in heaven. The Church is not here, it is there.

The Deliverance Promise

In Revelation 3, the church of Philadelphia is a prophetic picture of the true believing Church in the end days. Notice what it says in verse 10: "Because you have kept My command to persevere, I also will keep you from the hour of trial which shall come upon the whole world, to test those who dwell on the earth." This is a promise of deliverance from the time of testing.

There are some who tell us that during the Tribulation period, the Church will be here on earth and God will miraculously keep us safe like Shadrach, Meshach and Abed-Nego, preserved through the fire. But that is not what the Scripture says. The Bible doesn't say He will keep us from tribulation—it says He will keep us from the very hour of the Tribulation. We will not even see the time of the Tribulation period.

Paul presents the same truth in 1 Thessalonians 5:2: "The day of the Lord so comes as a thief in the night." The coming of a thief is unexpected and unannounced. Paul uses the illustration to show that it would be foolish for him to tell them when the tribulation would burst upon the world. He couldn't do that. It comes as a thief in the night. Then he goes on to tell them it isn't their concern anyway, because "You are all sons of light and sons of the day. We are not of the night nor of darkness" (v. 5). This tribulation period is a period for those in darkness. He further affirms, "For God did not appoint us to wrath, but to obtain salvation through our Lord Jesus Christ" (v. 9). The salvation he mentions here is not the saved-from-sin salvation, but a salvation or deliverance from the Tribulation period.

The Bible is so consistent. If part of God's divine program is to take His own out of judgment situations, wouldn't we also find that in the Old Testament? And we do.

Enoch was a godly man and walked with the Lord. God took him, He raptured him. The world was judged by a flood, but God took righteous Enoch out of the world.

Before Sodom and Gomorrah were judged and destroyed, Lot was taken out of Sodom. Lot asked to go to another city, and he was told by an angel, "Hurry, escape there. For I cannot do anything until you arrive there" (Genesis 19:22).

When God was going to slay the firstborn of the Egyptians, He made sure the godly people in the area were cared for with the blood on the door. They were saved before the judgement came.

Jericho was going to be destroyed. But before that happened, the spies and Rahab were taken out. The pattern of the Word of God is consistent from the beginning to the end. When judgment comes, God first of all removes His own.

Why? Because we have not been called to wrath, but to salvation. Jesus paid all the penalty for our sin. The Tribulation is a time of punitive judgment from God. If we have to go through it, that says what God did through Christ on the cross was not enough.

The Doctrine of Imminency

Do you believe Jesus could come back tonight? If you do, even if you don't understand it, you are pretribulational. Because if Jesus doesn't come back for the Rapture until the seven-year Tribulation is over, then He can't come back tonight. If He doesn't come back until three and a half years into the Tribulation period, He can't come back for at least three and a half years. The only doctrine in the Bible that is proven historically from the beginning all the way through is the doctrine of the imminency of Jesus Christ. Imminency means He could come back any time. One of the reasons I believe so strongly in the pretribulational view is that it is the only view consistent with the imminent return of Jesus Christ. The Bible teaches that the Christian waits in hope for the return of Christ. We are to be watching constantly for His return—He could come tonight.

Are you ready? You can't wait until Jesus comes back to make your decision. The Bible says in 2 Thessalonians 2:11-12 that people who have had a chance to hear the gospel during this age of grace will not have a legitimate chance for salvation after the Rapture. It says those who have heard the truth will be sent a strong delusion that they not believe the truth, because they had opportunity to accept the gospel of Christ and they rejected it. There will be people saved in the Tribulation period, but I don't believe there will be anyone saved who has heard the gospel in this age. You won't have a second chance. You've got one chance and it's now. Either you get ready or you get left.

APPLICATION

1. The following verses are read as prophetic Scriptures of the Tribulation.

Read Ezekiel 20:37-38. What do you think is the symbol for the Tribulation?

Read Micah 5:15. How does this relate to punishment of Gentile rejecters?

2. Read Revelation 4:1-4. What are the three significant things that suggest the twenty-four are symbolic representations of the Church?

Read the following verses:

Ephesians 2:6

2 Timothy 4:8

Revelation 19:8

Where is the Church at Revelation 4, the beginning of the Tribulation period?

3. Read Revelation 3:7-22. What is the problem with the church of Laodicea? Do you know anyone who seems to belong to this church?

Have you ever felt like a member of the church of Laodicea? If so, at what times? What was going on in your life? What circumstances, if any, brought you out of that state?

What command did the church of Philadelphia keep? Define that term in your own words.

Read Revelation 3:8. What does this verse mean to you? What do you think is in the promise of an open door?

4. Christians are not going to see the wrath of God in the Tribulation. Read the following verses:

Romans 5:9

Romans 8:1

1 Thessalonians 5:1-11

2 Thessalonians 1:3-10

How do we escape the wrath?

5. The Old Testament prefigures the New Testament, and the New Testament is interpreted in light of the Old Testament. Even the pictures of truth are consistent with the truth itself. Read the following passages:

Genesis 5:21-32; 6:5-8

Genesis 19:1-24

Exodus 11:1-7; 12:1-13

Joshua 6:1-25

Read 2 Peter 2:4-9. What is your previous knowledge of Lot?
What is God's opinion of Lot?

6. Read 2 Thessalonians 2:9-12. How does Paul put the reason for
the delusion God will send?

If Jesus came tonight, would you be ready?

If the answer is yes, what is your statement of faith?

If your answer is no, do you know what to do about it?

DID YOU KNOW?

In all of the Epistles in the New Testament, there is not one single statement to help Christians get ready for the future Tribulation. There are all kinds of statements about the problems we have now. The only reasonable answer for no instruction on this subject is because we will not be here. Otherwise the God who warned us about false teachers, and gave us this book to prepare us for things to come, would not leave out any encouragement or challenge or information to help us deal with the Tribulation we would be going to experience.

The Olivet Discourse Discussion

Selected Scriptures from Daniel

In this lesson we will see how the Olivet Discourse fits into the pretribulational position.

OUTLINE

A s we study Jesus' teaching on the Mount of Olives, we will learn the context of the teaching and which part of the end times Jesus is talking about.

   I. **The Passage Is Jewish**
  II. **The Passage Is a Response to Questions**
 III. **The Passage Is About Events to Come Before the Kingdom**
     A. The General Signs
     B. The Specific Signs
 IV. **The Post-Tribulation Position**
     A. Matthew 24:31
     B. Matthew 24:40-41
  V. **The Parable for Interpretation**

OVERVIEW

The Rapture for all intents and purposes is rendered inconsequential if it is post-tribulational. If the Lord Jesus is coming again immediately at the end of the Tribulation, why do the saints need to be raptured anyway? And if all believers are raptured and glorified just prior to the inauguration of the kingdom age, then there will be no one to populate and propagate the Kingdom. They will all be gone. Post-tribulationists teach a kind of yo-yo principle of the Rapture. They tell us at the end of the Tribulation we will go up and then come right back down. But there is no purpose for that, and no reason for it from the Scripture.

The character of God as a God of grace demands that the Church escape the Tribulation period because the majority of them have already escaped by dying. What good purpose could God have for a small group who just happen to be left at the end of time to be subjected to the Tribulation?

Another problem with the post-tribulation view is that there needs to be a period of time between the Rapture and the Second Advent of Jesus Christ in order for certain things to take place that are programmed in Scripture. The Bible teaches that during the Tribulation, the judgment seat of Christ will take place in heaven. Believers will be brought before the Bema seat to give an answer for the things done in the Body. The Marriage Supper of the Lamb will also convene during that time.

God's program is this: When the Church age is over, Christ will come and His own will be caught up to meet Him. The dead in Christ shall rise first, then those who are alive shall be caught up to be with the Lord. Immediately after that, the Tribulation period begins on earth; the judgment seat of Christ begins in heaven. For seven years the judgment of God against unbelieving Israel and Gentile rebels will take place on earth. At the end of that time, Christ will come back in His Second Coming, the Second Advent.

The difference between the Rapture and the Second Advent is that in the Rapture, Christ comes for His saints. In the Second Advent, Christ comes with His saints to reign on earth. If you don't distinguish between the two, you will always be confused about prophecy.

The Passage Is Jewish

Matthew 24 and 25, commonly referred to as the Olivet Discourse, is a passage of Scripture that deals with the Tribulation period. It has particular reference to the Jews. The sections of Matthew 24, Mark 13, Luke 17 and Luke 21 ought to be studied together. In these passages of Scripture, Jesus speaks to the Jewish people about preparation for Christ's return and the nature of the kingdom. These passages deal with questions the disciples asked. The disciples here are not representatives of the Church. They are representatives of Israel. In Matthew 24, the Church was not in the minds of the disciples. They didn't know about the Church or the Rapture yet.

Matthew 24 and 25 is a Jewish passage of Scripture. First of all, it takes place in Judea. In Matthew 24:20, it references a Jewish celebration, the Sabbath. In Matthew 24:15, it references the abomination prophesied by Daniel concerning the Jews. This concerns what will happen in the middle of the Tribulation when the Temple is desecrated. We often use the words "elect" to refer to the Church. But in this passage it is a reference to the Jews—those who are selected by God in a special way.

Luke 21 is dealing with God's message and place for the nation of Israel as He communicates it with the representatives of Jews, the disciples. The Church is not mentioned. The Rapture is not mentioned. There is no clear evidence that it is even in the minds of anybody in that discussion.

A Response to Questions

The Olivet Discourse was delivered by Christ during the last week before the crucifixion. In essence, it was a response to some questions that were asked Him by the disciples. The first question was, "When will the Temple be destroyed?" The second question was, "What will be the sign of Your coming?" The third question was, "What will be the sign of the end of the age?"

Christ answered the first question in another passage of Scripture. The prophecy was fulfilled in 70 A.D. when Jerusalem was destroyed and the Temple was flattened.

The last two questions have to do with the end time. It was not appropriate for Jesus Christ to speak directly of the Rapture at this time because the disciples were not prepared to understand it. Jesus had not instructed them about the Church yet, and it was not until the Apostle Paul that the full-blown truth of the Church was brought into existence. The Church was a mystery to them— "a truth that has been known from the beginning of time but has not yet been revealed," according to the New Testament meaning of "mystery." They could not understand the Rapture if they did not understand the Church, so there is no reason to expect it in this passage.

The disciples' first question indicates they were most concerned about when the Temple was going to be destroyed. The Temple was the most magnificent thing in the world in their day. If the Temple were to be destroyed, the world would be over as far as the Jews were concerned.

The end of the Temple would be synonymous with the end times, so their next questions were logical. "Lord, when the Temple is destroyed, then Your second coming must be shortly after that, and what is the sign? How shall we know when the end time comes?"

The coming of Christ and the end of the age are the same. But it is questionable if the disciples clearly understood at that time that there would be a period of time between the first coming and the second coming of Christ. The disciples were asking, "Lord, when are You going to come and establish Your Kingdom? We thought You were going to do it now, but You haven't done it. So when can we expect You to come back and do what we thought You were going to do when You were here the first time?"

Events to Come Before the Kingdom

The whole issue of Matthew 24 and 25 has nothing to do with the Rapture by specific reference. It has everything to do with the events that are going to come immediately before Christ comes to set up His Kingdom. The events that take place immediately before the Kingdom will be the Tribulation events. Since Jesus in this passage is teaching the disciples what would happen immediately before the Kingdom is established, He runs through the events of the Tribulation period.

The first thing Jesus does in Matthew 24 is to state the general signs that lead up to the second coming. He talks of people pretending to be Christ, of wars and rumors of wars, of famines and pestilence and earthquakes. He runs the events in front of them in panorama form. These are the events of the Tribulation period that immediately precede the Kingdom.

The second thing Jesus does is give the specific sign of the beginning of the Great Tribulation. The Great Tribulation is halfway through the Tribulation period. The Tribulation is bad, but the Great Tribulation is worse. The events which transpire in the last three and a half years are the worst events which take place in all of the world's history on this earth.

The specific thing that will happen before the beginning of the Great Tribulation is the abomination. Jesus says, "Therefore when you see the 'abomination of desolation,' spoken of by Daniel the prophet, standing in the holy place . . ." (Matthew 24:15), and then He goes on to describe what it will be like immediately before the Kingdom. He basically tells them it will be so awful they should run for their lives without looking back.

The details of the Tribulation are expanded upon in Revelation 4-18. What Jesus is teaching in Matthew 24 is not what will happen before the Rapture. The Lord is teaching the disciples, in answer to their questions, what will happen before the Kingdom is established. Some people are bothered that He doesn't mention the Rapture, but He had no reason to. He will give the disciples information about the Rapture in due time.

The Post-Tribulation Position

The post-tribulationists try to place the Church in Matthew 24 by referring to verse 31: "And He will send His angels with a great sound of a trumpet, and they will gather together His elect from the four winds, from one end of heaven to the other." The Bible teaches clearly that immediately before the Millennium starts there will be a gathering of the elect in preparation for the Millennium, but that is not the Rapture. There is no mention here of the translation of any saints. There is not one word concerning a resurrection. 1 Thessalonians 4 tells us that associated with the Rapture is the resurrection of those who are dead in Christ. There is nothing here that has the earmark of the Rapture. It is simply a reference to the final gathering of the elect before the millennial period begins.

Another place post-tribulationists try to insinuate the Rapture into this chapter is in verses 40-42: "Then two men will be in the field: one will be taken and the other left. Two women will be grinding at the mill: one will be taken and the other left. Watch therefore, for you do not know what hour your Lord is coming." The Bible teaches that the Rapture will be like this. But this passage does not speak of the Rapture. A few verses earlier, the word for "taken" was used to explain how those not saved by the flood at the time of Noah were taken. How were they taken? They were taken in judgment, not in Rapture. When the flood came, those who had rejected Noah's message were not raptured. They were taken away by the flood in judgment. What this passage is teaching is that in the day of the Tribulation when the Lord comes in judgment upon this earth, some will be judged like that, independently, immediately. There won't be a mass judgment totally across the whole world, but independent individuals will be judged. One will be judged, another left.

The companion passage in Luke 17 ends with Jesus' answer to the disciples' question about where they would be taken: "Wherever the body is, there the eagles will be gathered together" (v. 37). He was talking about the vultures that are going to get their carcasses in judgment, not the Rapture.

The Parable for Interpretation

The parable that our Lord used is the key as to how we interpret this passage for today in advance of these events. He said, "Now learn this parable from the fig tree: When its branch has already become tender and puts forth leaves, you know that summer is near. So you also, when you see all these things, know that it is near—at the doors!" (Matthew 24:32-33).

We do not know the exact times and seasons, but I do believe the Bible teaches that we can know when we are nearing the time of the end of all things. Jesus was teaching His disciples a valid principle of Bible interpretation—coming events cast their shadows before them. I don't mean to suggest there are signs that need to be fulfilled before the Rapture can take place, but the Lord does say that if you study Scripture and look at God's movements and the affairs of humanity, you will have some indication of when God is setting the stage that will consummate in the Second Coming of the Son of God.

One of the signs Jesus said would come to pass before the kingdom was set up is famines. There are famines today all over this globe. I personally believe the next great crisis will be universal famine. All you have to do is ponder the population explosion.

It is not wrong to say the signs are telling us the Lord's coming draws nigh. It is wrong to say that all of these things happen and then the Rapture comes. That's not what this passage is teaching.

What prophecy does for you more than anything else is give you a perspective on the future, a certain knowledge that Christ is in control. He has a plan and a program. He might come today, but if He doesn't, I am going to live my life to the fullest, accomplishing what He has given me to do. Jesus is coming again.

APPLICATION

1. The Bible teaches that after the Church is raptured and goes to heaven, the judgment seat of Christ will take place in heaven for the believers. Read the following verses:

John 5:24-30

Romans 14:10-12

2 Corinthians 5:10

1 Thessalonians 4:15-17

2 Timothy 4:8

What things do you think you will have to answer for at the Judgment?

How is it possible to be judged and not "come into judgment"?

2. Matthew 24-25 is a Jewish passage of Scripture. Read Matthew 24:20. How is this a specifically Jewish reference?

Read Colossians 2:13-17, 20-23. How has Christ "changed the rules"?

3. Read Matthew 24:1-3. What are the disciples asking about the Temple?

What was the importance of the Temple to the Jewish people and to Christ? Read the following verses:

Ezra 5:7-17

Habakkuk 2:20

Matthew 12:3-6

Matthew 27:50-51

John 2:13-17

4. Read Matthew 24:3-14. Make a list of the things Jesus says will happen at the end of the age.

Read Matthew 24:9. Who will be delivered up to Tribulation?

5. Read Matthew 24:32-33.

What is Jesus saying in this parable?

Look back at the list you wrote in answer to question 4. How many of these things do you see happening today?

6. John Powell said that when you suppress things you don't want to live with, you don't really solve the problem because you don't bury the problem dead—you bury the problem alive. Does this relate at all to how you feel about the problems that will come near the end of the age?

What does prophecy do for your perspective on the future?

DID YOU KNOW?

It took all of recorded history for the world to produce its first billion inhabitants around 1850. In other words, from creation until 1850, it took that long to produce the first billion inhabitants on this globe. It took 80 years to pass the two billion mark in 1930. It took another 31 years to reach 3 billion in 1961. But only 15 years were required to add the fourth billion by 1976. Those who have studied the situation tell us if we continue to grow at our present rate, in 900 years we will have 60 million billion people on the earth. That's 100 people for every square yard of earth, land or sea.

Superpowers in Conflict

Daniel 8:1-8, 15-21

In this lesson we will look at the many facets of Daniel's second vision.

OUTLINE

As we study the second vision of Daniel, we will examine some introductory truth about it, and we will see what the vision actually communicates. We will also look at a great principle concerning our response to the Bible.

I. **The Reception of Daniel's Second Vision**
   A. The Position of the Vision
   B. The Profile of the Vision
   C. The Place of the Vision
   D. The Purpose of the Vision
   E. The Paraphrase of the Vision
   F. The Plan of the Vision
II. **The Revelation of Daniel's Second Vision**
   A. The Ram
   B. The Goat
III. **The Resolution of Daniel's Second Vision**
   A. A Great Prophecy
   B. A Great Principle
   C. A Great Person

OVERVIEW

Quite often when I talk to people who are not students of the Bible, they focus on the strange nature of biblical information. They say things like, "The Bible is really a weird book. Take Daniel—there are animals everywhere. You read the Book of Revelation, there are all kinds of weird symbols and signs and animals there. How in the world is anybody supposed to understand anything when they're trying to tell great truth by using animals? I mean, nobody ever uses animals in communication."

But the fact is, we do. Sometimes we look back on the times when the Scripture was being written and think: They just communicated in a different way than we do today. But is it really that different? What about these statements?

> My grandfather is as wise as an owl.
> He eats like a horse.
> I know I should stand up to her, but I guess I'm
> just chicken.
> She has the memory of an elephant.
> Sometimes he's as dumb as an ox.
> My husband is as stubborn as a mule.

Isn't it interesting to realize communication hasn't changed all that much? As we study the eighth chapter, we will discover that the animals in this story are unique because they have a special meaning in the time in which this prophecy was written.

The Reception of Daniel's Second Vision

The Position of the Vision

Daniel 8 records the second vision that Daniel personally received. Let me remind you that Daniel is put together in two sections. Chapters one through six are history. Chapters seven through twelve are prophecies that were received during the time of the first six chapters. Daniel's vision in chapter eight actually took place chronologically between the fourth and fifth chapters. That is important to understand, because what God communicates to Daniel in the eighth chapter prepares him to understand what he needs to know when he walks on the scene in the fifth chapter.

This vision came to Daniel just before the tragic events of the end of the Babylonian Empire. What Daniel saw in the vision helped him to know how to decipher the handwriting on the wall.

This second vision came to Daniel in about 550 or 549 B.C. At that point in time Daniel was about sixty to sixty-seven years old. Two years elapsed between the vision he had in chapter seven and the vision in chapter eight.

The Profile of the Vision

In Daniel 2, God gave Daniel the whole panorama of Gentile history from the time of Babylon to the end times, even to the divided Roman Empire in the future. He communicated this as a gigantic beast. In chapter eight, God zooms in on the middle section of that image. We will see just the arms, shoulders, and torso. Chapter eight isn't about Babylon or Rome. It's about the Persians and the Medes and the Greeks.

The entire focus from now on in Daniel is on the Gentile powers only as they relate to the Jews. There aren't any nations more important in the study of the history of Israel than the Persians and the Greeks. It was under the Persian government that the Jews were allowed to return from Babylon and set up their land again and worship. It was under the Greeks that the Temple and the city were ultimately destroyed.

In the original language of the Old Testament, there is a change of language in chapter eight. In chapters two through seven, the language is Aramaic, the Gentile language of the day. In the eighth chapter, Hebrew is used once again because the coming events foretold will affect the Jews.

In Daniel 8:9, there is a name that gives a clue to the significance of the Israelites in this prophecy. "And out of one of them came a little horn which grew exceedingly great toward the south, toward the east, and toward the Glorious Land." The Glorious Land is Israel.

The Place of the Vision

When the prophecy came to Daniel, he was transported in his vision to Shushan, the city of the palace. At that particular time, Shushan was a little, insignificant city at the fringe area of the Babylonian kingdom—an unknown place with absolutely no significance to the Babylonian kingdom. Later on it became the very nerve center of the next kingdom. Daniel is in the very center of that prophecy in his mind's eye.

The Purpose of the Vision

The purpose of this vision was to prepare Daniel for the end of the Babylonian kingdom and help him know what to say and do when he walked into the drunken party and saw the handwriting on the wall. It helped him understand that God was saying to Belshazzar that the Babylonian kingdom was over. The Medes and Persians were on their way. It was doomsday for Babylon. The next dynasty was about to begin.

Daniel was told the vision was about the time of the end. God was not just talking about the end of that particular time. He was positioning Himself to tell Daniel about the end of time itself, when the kingdoms of this world will be assimilated into the kingdom of our God.

The Paraphrase of the Vision

Daniel was emotionally involved in the vision God gave him. In fact, he became so emotional that he fainted and was sick for several days. He didn't know what the vision meant, so God sent someone to tell him what it meant. He didn't send just anybody; He sent Gabriel. When God had something special to share, He dispatched Gabriel.

The Plan of the Vision

God didn't send unorganized visions to His prophets. He always planned them so the prophets would understand exactly what was going on. In essence, God was teaching Daniel what is ultimately the truth concerning the man whom we know as the Antichrist. But in order for God to get the message through to Daniel, He gave it to him in a threefold measure. He looks out into the future with a king "having fierce features" (Daniel 8:23). That is the Antichrist. Then He gives Daniel two earlier persons in history who are pictures of the Antichrist. Each of these three personages is labeled as a horn: the big horn, the little horn and the final horn. In Daniel, the word "horn" stands for king or power or kingdom. These three horns are three kings.

The Revelation of Daniel's Second Vision

The Ram

The first animal Daniel saw was a ram with two horns. The horns are explained in verse twenty as the kings of Media and Persia. The ram is the Medo-Persian Empire. The prophecy meticulously describes one of the horns as being higher than the other, and the higher one came up last. This shows how the Medes came first and were joined by the Persians. The Persian Empire assimilated the Median Empire just as the prophecy showed.

The Goat

The first colony of Greece was established by an oracle that sent a goat for a guide to build a city in an unknown place. The goat came to the region of Greece. In gratitude for the goat leading them in the right direction, the city was built and called "aegae," meaning goat. The goat was Greece.

In Daniel 8:5-7 are five of the most amazing prophecies I have ever studied, amazingly fulfilled down to the minutest detail. The first prophecy has to do with the route to world conquest of the Greeks. It says when the goat began to move out of the west and cover the whole earth, it moved so rapidly that it didn't touch the ground. When the Greek Empire began to grow, conquests amassed so quickly that Greece set world records for bringing the world under its dominion. In twelve brief years, the Greeks conquered the entire civilized world, never losing a battle. God said that was how it would happen before it ever took place.

The second amazing prophecy has to do with the reputation of the king. The Scripture says that the horn in the middle of the forehead of the goat was the first king of Greece (see v. 21). Who was the first king of Greece? Alexander the Great. Alexander was the son of Philip of Macedon and of Olympia. When Alexander was growing up, his mother taught him he was a descendant of Achilles and Hercules. His father was a great militarist and leader. Yet he told his son, "Alexander, my son, seek out a kingdom worthy of yourself. Macedonia is too small for you." Alexander went for the world and got it. I wonder how much of that was built into him because of the faith his parents had in him.

The third prophecy has to do with the ruin of the Medo-Persian Empire. God told Daniel when the notable horn, the great king, came to power, he would go against the Persians and the Medes.

When Alexander finally decided to take the Medes and Persians down, he came with 35,000 troops from the west, defeated the Persian army under Darius III, and freed all of the Greek cities of Asia Minor from the Persians. He refused to negotiate with Darius, swept on south, took Egypt, Tyre, Gaza, then retraced his steps through Syria and met an enlarged Persian army. This time he wiped out the Medo-Persian Empire just like God said he would, two hundred years before it happened.

The fourth amazing prophecy has to do with the remarkable death of the king. When Alexander conquered the Medo-Persians, he sacked several other Persian cities and swept on to India, but his tired army had had enough and they returned to Babylon where Alexander died at the age of thirty-three. He was a victim of his own drunkenness and fever, depressed in his own spirit because there weren't any more worlds for him to conquer. When he was strong at the height of his glory, the great horn was broken (see v. 8).

The last great prophecy of this chapter has to do with the reorganization of the Greek Empire. The prophecy said that when Alexander died his kingdom would be divided in four, given to four kings who were not as strong as Alexander, and the power of the total kingdom would be dissipated. For twenty years after Alexander's death there was all kinds of struggling and infighting. Within that period of time the kingdom of Alexander was divided between four of his generals. All of this was written long before it ever happened.

The Resolution of Daniel's Second Vision

This is a great prophecy. Here is prophecy written down about things we now know took place exactly as God said they would. The Antichrist hasn't come yet, but he will. When you study prophecy, you see how literally it is fulfilled.

Here is a great principle. Daniel's reaction to the prophecy was emotional, even physical. We usually respond to God's Word by taking it for granted. I believe God would have us get serious about His Book as Daniel did. When we read about the coming Antichrist who is going to devastate those who have been left behind, we should begin to look around for those who don't know Jesus Christ and ask God to help us get them in the kingdom before His prophecy comes true.

This prophecy introduces a great man. Alexander was a powerful man, a great dictator and ruler, a great general and leader. It's easy to compare him to another great One who died at thirty-three. By all of the standards of humanism and world history, Alexander stands rank and file above our Lord. But there's not a person who has ever walked with Jesus for one day who would debate the issue for a moment. Jesus is the greatest!

APPLICATION

1. Long before the Persian Empire was ever begun, long before the Babylonians even knew the Persians were a threat to their kingdom, long before Daniel 5 when Babylon fell, God spoke to Daniel and in a vision transported him to the very nerve center of the next kingdom. Read the following verses:

Daniel 8:1-2

Nehemiah 1:1-2

Esther 1:1-4

Using a study Bible, find out when King Artaxerxes (see Nehemiah 2:1) and King Ahasuerus reigned. How does this time compare to the time of Daniel's second vision?

Why is it significant that God gave Daniel the vision about Shushan before Shushan mattered?

2. Read the following verses:

Daniel 8:1

Daniel 8:15

Daniel 8:17

Daniel 8:27

What clues in these verses reveal Daniel's reaction? What do these verses tell about Daniel's involvement in what God was communicating to him?

What is your general involvement and reaction when you read the Bible? When you read prophecy?

3. Read Daniel 8:3-8. Below, write the literal meaning of each of these symbols:

Verse 3— the ram

        the higher horn

        the lower horn

Verse 5— the goat

Verse 8— the large horn

After Alexander died, his kingdom was divided between his four generals—Cassander, Lysimachus, Seleucus and Ptolemy. How does this fit into the prophecy?

4. In the Old Testament, the word "gbr" means "the mighty one." One of the names for God is "el." So the name for Gabriel, "gbrel" means "the mighty one of God." Read the following verses about this angel.

Daniel 8:16-19

Daniel 9:21-22

Luke 1:11-19

Luke 1:26-38

In the Bible, only two angels (other than Lucifer) are called by name, Gabriel and Michael. What do you think is the significance of that?

5. Charles Ross Weed has written a poem comparing and stating the dissimilarities between Alexander the Great and Jesus Christ. Do some comparing yourself and write what Jesus did in contrast to each of Alexander's exploits.

Alexander	Jesus
lived and died for himself	
died on a throne	
shed a whole world's blood	
made all men slaves	
is dead forever	

DID YOU KNOW?

I n the Bible, Israel is called Canaan, the Holy Land, the Lord's land, Emmanuel's land, land of Israel, land of the Hebrews, land of Judah, land of Promise, land of Palestine and the Pleasant or Glorious Land.

Antiochus and the Antichrist

Daniel 8:9-14, 22-27

In this lesson we will see how Antiochus Epiphanes was a type of the Antichrist.

OUTLINE

As we study the second vision of Daniel, we will examine the cruelty of Antiochus Epiphanes and the cruelty of the coming Antichrist.

   I. **Antiochus Epiphanes**
  II. **Antichrist—Characteristics**
    A. Dramatic in Appearance
    B. Destined to do Evil
    C. Dynamic Leadership
    D. Demonic in Power
    E. Destructive in His Reign
    F. Deceitful in His Practice
    G. Deifies Himself
    H. Disguises His Cruelty with Peace Promises
    I. Destroyed Without Human Hands

OVERVIEW

When Daniel speaks of the Antichrist who is coming and the antichrists who have come, that is not an empty prophecy. It is a truth validated by the mail I receive. Parts of one letter written to me said, "I am the one God has sent to be the return of Christ. Ask the F.B.I. I have proven it to them as well as to many others. . . . We are a team, God, Jesus and myself. We are the Holy Trinity whether you believe it or not, and if you don't, to hell with you! We don't need you, you need us. . . . If you have any intentions of getting to heaven it must be through me, for I am here now and doing God's will, and I have that say so, and I say that you shall never go to heaven unless and until you recognize me. I am the second Christ. Make no mistake about that."

This guy is serious. He has come to the conclusion that in his lifetime he is the one Christ has sent. He believes he is Jesus Christ. The Bible says there are many coming who will say they are Christ. Daniel's prophecy in the eighth chapter is to the effect that there is an Antichrist coming.

Antiochus Epiphanes

Daniel 8 is built around three people: two people of historical significance and one prophetic individual. The notable or great horn was Alexander the Great. He illustrates the power of the coming Antichrist. He is followed in the text by the little horn. He came out of one of the kingdoms ruled over by one of Alexander's generals. We know now that was Seleucus's kingdom. Scripture records him as "a little horn which grew exceedingly great" (v. 9). The prophecy is fulfilled in a person history knows as Antiochus Epiphanes. His name means "Antiochus God Manifest" or "Antiochus the great one of God."

According to history, he persecuted people. In Egypt, when he was on his way to conquer the world, he was stopped by the armies of Rome. In fury and frustration, Antiochus turned his forces away from Egypt and marched up through the maritime border of the Mediterranean. He vented his anger by taking his army to Jerusalem and sacking the city. During that march, Antiochus killed some 50,000 Jews. He took 40,000 of the people and sold them into slavery. He also plundered the temple. He took the golden altar of incense and stood before the inner veil. He decided to destroy the Jewish religion and substitute for it Greek worship and Greek culture.

Instead of the Feast of the Tabernacles, Antiochus Epiphanes celebrated in the Temple the feast of Bacchanalia, worshipping Bacchus, the god of pleasure and wine. He forced the Jews to observe the Saturnalia, worshipping Saturn, using harlots in the Temple for those feast days. He forbade the observance of the Sabbath. He not only forbade the reading of the Scriptures, he burned every copy of the Torah he could find. Any Jewish practice was forbidden on penalty of death. He did everything he could to desecrate and destroy their religion forever.

Antiochus forced the Jews to observe all of his feast days and forbade the institution of circumcision. History records in the Book of Maccabees that there were two mothers, deeply committed to their Jewish culture, who determined to circumcise their boys. When Antiochus heard about it, he took the babies and killed them, hung them around each mother's neck, marched the women through the city streets of Jerusalem up to the highest wall and flung them, babies and all, headlong over the wall.

One mother who had seven sons defied Antiochus' law. Antiochus cut the tongues out of the boys' mouths and then fried the boys to death, one at a time, on a flatiron. Then he murdered the mother. This is just a short vignette of a long history of agony under Antiochus Epiphanes. He tried to strip every semblance of the Jewish faith from the Jews.

When the Scripture speaks of the desecration of the Temple (see Daniel 8:13), it is speaking of the time Antiochus walked into the sacred place of the Jews with a sow. He slit the throat of the sow and sacrificed the pig on the altar of the Jewish people. Then he took the juice from that animal and sprayed it all over the inside of the Temple. Everything that was holy to the Jews had sow's blood all over it.

In a vision, Daniel heard a holy one ask another holy one how long it would go on. The reply was 2,300 days, or literally, evening and mornings. Scholars differ in their understanding of that terminology. If we take the 2,300 evenings/mornings to represent morning sacrifice and evening sacrifice, we get 1,250 days. That fits, although not exactly, into the three and a half years of the first half of the Tribulation. If we take the 2,300 as full days, that fits the seven year period, but not exactly.

The atrocities of Antiochus did end. There was living in those days a priest in a place called Modein, just outside of Jerusalem. The priest's name was Mattathias. He was a patriarch and grieved over the sorrow of his people. One day an emissary from Antiochus came to Modin to make the Jews bow down before the altar of Jupiter, the Greek god. When a Jew came to worship Jupiter, Mattathias killed him, then he killed the officer that made the Jew bow down. And the Maccabean revolt was on. Mattathias was old and died before the revolt was over. He passed his torch on to his third son, Judas Maccabaeus, who won the victory of Antiochus and independence for the Jews.

When Judas Maccabaeus went back in to cleanse the Temple, he wanted to light the lamps in the Temple. The ceremony to reconsecrate the Temple required eight days, but he only found enough oil for one day. Tradition says the one cruse of oil lasted not only for the first day, it lasted throughout all eight days. In celebration of that miraculous reconsecration of the Temple, the Jewish people celebrate Hanukkah.

Antichrist

As the leadership of Alexander demonstrates the power of the coming Antichrist, Antiochus Epiphanes demonstrates the cruelty of the coming Antichrist. In Daniel 8:23 we see the final person, the one toward whom all of this prophetic information is pointing. God prophesied concerning Alexander and Antiochus, and history validates the prophecy. These were real people. Just as those two men of history came to pass, the prophecy concerning the Antichrist will literally come to pass. The stage is being set even now. The interesting thing is that the characteristics of these other two men merge together in what we learn about the king with fierce features, the Antichrist.

Dramatic in Appearance

When the Antichrist comes at the end of time, he will be dramatic in appearance. In the latter time of their kingdom, when the climactic time has come, when everything has happened that points to the advance of evil, the king of fierce countenance will make his appearance. Every prophetic truth in the Old and New Testaments has some relationship to the coming of the Antichrist.

Destined to Do Evil

The Scripture says that the Antichrist will come "when the transgressors have reached their fullness" (v. 23). When evil is at its worst, when things are happening you can't even imagine happening, when all the restraints are lifted and everything seems to be going full-blown in the direction of evil and Satan, at that moment the Antichrist will walk across the scene.

Dynamic Leadership

Verse twenty-three says the king will arise "who understands sinister schemes." This refers both to his ability to solve problems and to his dynamic leadership. He will be a man who will walk into the frame of reference of our world and have all the right answers. Some expositors believe this matter of "dark sayings" (KJV) is a reference to the fact that he will be involved with the occult.

Demonic in Power

Verse twenty-four says, "His power shall be mighty, but not by his own power." That means he will be demonic, demon-possessed. Revelation 13:2 says the Dragon gave to Antichrist his power and his seat and his great authority. In the future, when the Antichrist walks on this earth, he will be indwelt by Satan. I can't help but believe that Antiochus Epiphanes must have been Satan-filled in order to commit the atrocities he did. He was demonic just as the Antichrist will be.

Destructive in His Reign

"He shall destroy fearfully" (Daniel 8:24). The whole world will wonder at his destructiveness. And he will "prosper and thrive; he shall destroy the mighty, and also the holy people." Antiochus did this. Alexander did this. And the Antichrist will do it. In the prophecies concerning the Tribulation period, there are times when blood is let to such a degree it is up to the level of the bridles of the horses. The stench of fallen flesh will be so great that when the ships pass the harbor from the place where the battles are fought, those sailing will have to stop their noses because of the overwhelming odor. Everything I know about Antiochus Epiphanes causes me to shudder, but when I think the Antichrist will be that man multiplied a hundred times over, I cannot imagine the evil that will run rampant on this earth during that seven-year period.

Deceitful in His Practice

"Through his cunning he shall cause deceit to prosper under his rule" (v. 25). The Antichrist will come telling everyone he is God and doing lying wonders. The Antichrist will be the great deceiver. He will come with lies and wonders and deceive the people, just as Antiochus did.

Deifies Himself

On the coins printed during Antiochus' reign were the words, "Theos Antiochus Theos Epiphanes." That means, "Antiochus the Great, God Manifest." He said he was God, just like the Antichrist will when he comes. He will deify himself.

Disguises His Cruelty with Peace Promises

"And by peace he shall destroy many" (v. 25, KJV). There is coming a day when the Antichrist, in order to make peace with the Jews, will make a covenant with them at the beginning of the tribulation period. He'll promise them they can worship and observe their feast days. He'll gain their confidence by deceit and then break the covenant. All hell will break out. That will usher in the Great Tribulation, the time of great suffering on this earth.

Antiochus Epiphanes portrays this quality in the coming Antichrist. First Maccabees 1:29-30 says, "And after two years' time the king Antiochus sent his chief collector of tribute into the cities of Judah, and he came into Jerusalem, and he spake words of peace unto them in deceit, and they gave him credence and he fell suddenly upon the city and smote it very sore and destroyed much of the people of Israel." Promises of peace followed by destruction.

Destroyed Without Human Hand

The Antichrist will be "broken without human means" (Daniel 8:25). He will be supernaturally killed. Even in this Antiochus Epiphanes illustrates the Antichrist. He made great strides in his godless purge until finally, because the Jews had cast the image of Jupiter out of the Temple, he became embittered and claimed he would make Jerusalem a common burial place. No sooner had

Antiochus made this declaration than he was afflicted with an incurable disease. His sufferings were unbearable and the stench from his own body was so horrible even Antiochus couldn't stand the smell. Finding it impossible to fulfill his threat, he frankly confessed that he knew he was suffering because of what he had done to the Jews and their worship. He died in misery, a foolish man who thought he could resist God and get away with it. He was brought down supernaturally without a human hand touching him.

How does that apply to the Antichrist? He will not end naturally, either. One day King Jesus will ride out of glory and go into combat with that old boy. The end of it will be that the Antichrist will be cast into hell.

APPLICATION

1. First Maccabees 1:44-50 says, "And the king Antiochus sent letters by messengers unto Jerusalem and the cities of Judah that they should follow the foreign customs of the land and keep burnt offerings and sacrifices and drink offerings out of the sanctuary, and that they should profane the sabbaths and the festival days, and pollute the sanctuary and priests, and build altars and graves and idol temples, and sacrifice swine's flesh and unclean animals, and that they should leave souls abominable with all manner of uncleanness and profanation to the end that they might forget the law and change the ordinances."

What were Antiochus's purposes for his actions and his declarations?

The Jews called Antiochus Epiphanes, Antiochus Epimanes. That means, "Antiochus the madman." Do you think there will be an alternate name for the Antichrist when he comes?

2. Read Daniel 8:11. What do you know of Antiochus Epiphanes that goes along with this prophecy?

Read 2 Thessalonians 2:3-4. How does this prophecy of the Antichrist mesh with the Daniel prophecy?

Read Ezekiel 28:2, 6-8. What generally happens to people who set themselves up as God?

3. The Antichrist will be demonic and destructive. Read the following verses:

Daniel 8:24

Revelation 13:2

Revelation 13:4-7

Read Matthew 24:21-22. What in your opinion have been the worst times in history in terms of cruelty toward, and slaughter of, humanity?

Can you imagine happenings so bad that nothing in history can compare to them?

4. Read Daniel 8:27. Here are some clues regarding what our response should be to this story about persecution and the coming Antichrist.

What was Daniel's reaction to the prophecy?

Why do you think he responded that way?

How would you respond if you knew your loved ones would go through something as awful as these things described?

Are any of your loved ones outside of Christ? If so, who?

5. What is our responsibility as Christians to unbelievers?

How seriously do you take your own responsibility?

Read the following verses:

Daniel 12:1-3

Matthew 28:18-20

Romans 1:15-16

2 Timothy 4:1-5

6. Prophecy is only good when it has a direct application to what is going on right now. Read 1 Thessalonians 5:20. If you really believe what you have studied in this chapter, how will it change your life?

DID YOU KNOW?

I n the Douay version of the Bible, which Catholics use, there is a section called the Apocrypha. In that Apocryphal section there are two books called 1 and 2 Maccabees. These two books are the history of the inter-testament period, the 400 silent years from the end of the Old Testament to the New. Those two books record many of the events spoken of in this chapter. They are not inspired in that they are not Scripture, but they are accurate history of the period of time. They are also supported by the historian Josephus.

God's Word and Prayer

Daniel 9:1-4

In this lesson we will learn some principles of prayer.

OUTLINE

As we study Daniel's prayer in the ninth chapter, we will see it as an illustration of what praying ought to be. We will examine its relationship to the Bible and our lives.

   I. Life-Changing Prayer Is Motivated by the Word of God
  II. Life-Changing Prayer Is Measured by the Will of God
 III. Life-Changing Prayer Is Manifested in Our Walk with God
     A. Frequency of Prayer
     B. Fervency of Prayer

L eonard Ravenhill has written of the Church, "We have many organizers, but few agonizers. We have many players and payers, but few prayers. We have many singers, but few clingers. Lots of pastors, but few wrestlers. Many fears, few tears. Much fashion, but little passion. Many interferers, but far too few intercessors. Many writers, but few fighters. Failing here, we fail everywhere."

That's hard to take because it's true. And that's why, when we come to a passage on prayer, we had better listen, because here God has something to say to us that can change that decay in our lives and in our church.

The ninth chapter of the Book of Daniel contains one of the greatest Old Testament prayers. In many respects, this illustration of prayer in the midst of prophecy is like an oasis in the middle of a desert. It is an example of what praying ought to be. Also in this chapter is the well-known prophecy of the seventy weeks. But the prophecy which gives this chapter its fame is two times shorter than the prayer which precedes it. I really believe we cannot understand the prophecy and its significance until we get into the prayer.

Life-Changing Prayer Is Motivated by the Word of God

When Daniel went into captivity with the rest of the Jews, he didn't have a copy of the Bible like we have today. There was obviously no New Testament, and vast portions of the Old Testament were not available. But when Daniel went into captivity, he did have some portions of the Old Testament. In particular, he had some of the writings of Jeremiah the Prophet.

Jeremiah ministered in the time just previous to the captivity of the people of Judah. He was the last prophet to call out to those people to repent before the judgment of God fell upon them. Isaiah had prophesied many years earlier, and they wouldn't listen, but right up until the very last moment, Jeremiah cried out against the sin of Judah and called them to repentance. But they would not repent, and they were all carried away into captivity.

When Daniel was about eighty-five or eighty-six, he was reading in Jeremiah and I believe something jumped off the page into his heart that motivated his prayer in chapter nine. It must have been Jeremiah 25:8-11: "Therefore thus says the LORD of hosts: 'Because you have not heard My words, behold, I will send and take all the families of the north,' says the LORD, 'and Nebuchadnezzar the king of Babylon, My servant, and will bring them against this land, against its inhabitants, and against these nations all around, and will utterly destroy them, and make them an astonishment, a hissing, and perpetual desolations. Moreover I will take from them the voice of mirth and the voice of gladness, the voice of the bridegroom and the voice of the bride, the sound of the millstones and the light of the lamp. And this whole land shall be a desolation and an astonishment.'"

Daniel knew all about this. He had lived through almost seventy years of it. From the very beginning Daniel had watched as the song had been taken out of the hearts of his people as they hung their harps on the willows and cried out for the day when they could go back to Jerusalem. He saw their captivity take the very life out of their Jewish culture and history. But that's not the part of the prophecy that caught Daniel's attention. It was the last part of verse eleven and following: "'And these nations shall serve the king of Babylon seventy years. Then it will come to pass, when seventy years are completed, that I will punish the king of Babylon and that nation, the land of the Chaldeans, for their iniquity,' says the LORD; 'and I will make it a perpetual desolation. So I will bring on that land all My words which I have pronounced against it, all that is written in this book, which Jeremiah has prophesied concerning all the nations. (For many nations and great kings shall be served by them also; and I will repay them according to their deeds and according to the works of their own hands.)'"

Daniel was in his early to mid-eighties at the time, depending on how old he was when he was taken captive. Now as he reads the prophecy of Jeremiah he knows that almost seventy years have come to pass since he was carried away captive with the people. The prophecy gets hold of his heart because he begins to realize the time for the return of his people to Jerusalem is drawing near. He probably does not know whether the time is calculated from the first, second, or third deportation. But he does know the time is getting close. It's almost time for God to redeem His people and take them back to their land. The prophecy got such a hold on Daniel's heart, he fell on his knees and began to pray.

Isn't it true that when we really come to grips with prophecy, it ought to have that kind of effect on us? Yet we so often get caught up in the exercise of understanding prophetic truth that we miss the whole point. The point of prophetic truth is that it ought to drive us to our knees even as it did Daniel. When Daniel read what God had to say, he couldn't stay the same. His prayer was motivated by the Word of God.

I think it is always proper before we open the Scripture to briefly ask for God's blessing and insight into the text. But if I understand the priority of the Word of God, prayer grows out of God's Word. When we read the Word of God and study it, as we come to grips with what it means, we find within us a prayer being formed that will take the Word of God and apply it to our very experience.

Life-Changing Prayer Is Measured by the Will of God

Daniel read in the Book of Jeremiah that God was going to keep his people in captivity for seventy years, and then He was going to release them. A strange thing happens as he reads what God is going to do. He begins to pray that God will do what He's going to do. Basically he prays, "Lord, what You said You were going to do, that's what I want You to do."

If God has said He's going to do something, why should we pray? God knows His plan, and even when He reveals His plan to us, He expects us to pray over that plan. God revealed that His time was about up for the captive people. When Daniel got the truth about what God would do, he fell to his knees and began to pray in the will of God that God would do what He was going to do.

Sometimes I get the impression, even from my own prayers, that we have misunderstood the meaning of prayer. Prayer is not to get God to change His will. If you really believe that the will of God is perfect, then why would you want Him to change it? But we labor long at prayer trying to get God to change His will from what we think He is going to do, when our prayer really ought to be motivated out of our deep understanding of what the will of God is.

The will of God will never lead you contrary to the Word of God. When your prayer is motivated by the Word of God and you understand what God has said, then you can pray what God has already said to be His will. Prayer is not a device for getting our will done through heaven. It is a device for allowing God's will to be done on earth through us. That's why we are told to pray, "Thy kingdom come, Thy will be done." Prayer is not getting God to adjust His program to what we want. Prayer is adjusting our lives to the revealed will of God. When we pray, it isn't God who changes— it's us.

Life-Changing Prayer Is Manifested in Our Walk with God

Frequency of Prayer

There are two things about Daniel's life that come into focus when we examine his praying. First of all, there is his frequency of prayer. Prayer shouldn't just be something we do at a point in time. Prayer should be a part of our total life and being. In Daniel, prayer is the very fabric of his life.

Daniel 6:10 is a testimony to the frequency of Daniel's praying. When he knew there was a law against praying to anyone other than Darius, he went home and prayed, "as was his custom since early days." When the crisis came, Daniel didn't change anything. He kept right on doing what he had always done. Maybe one of those prayers he prayed is this prayer in chapter nine.

Fervency of Prayer

Daniel's praying wasn't like ours so often is. He didn't see God as a divine bellhop to get him whatever he needed at a moment's notice. He didn't pop in front of God and say his thing and leave. Daniel was fervent in prayer.

What does it mean to be fervent in prayer? In the Old Testament culture there were certain things that accompanied fervent prayer. The emotional involvement of a person who was praying fervently for the will of God to be done might include any of the following: The person might wear sackcloth (the garments of mourning), sit in an ash pile, put ashes on his head, or shave off the hair on his head. They may smite their breast, cry, tear their garments, fast, sigh, groan, sweat blood, agonize, pour out their heart, make oaths or sacrifices. Somehow our prayer lives don't seem to fit into that context. That's fervent praying.

Another element of fervent praying may involve fasting. Jesus fasted. Paul fasted. Early church leaders fasted. In the Old Testament, Isaiah, Daniel, Esther, David, Hannah, Elijah, Ezra, Nehemiah, Zechariah, and others fasted. In church history you learn that Martin Luther, John Calvin, John Knox, John and Charles Wesley, David Brainerd, George Mueller, and many more fasted. It's hard to find a great person of faith who didn't fast.

We are not commanded to fast in the New Testament. But that does not do away with the fact that sometimes fasting gets at this matter of fervency in our praying. It is a time in our lives when we say "No" to our physical wants and desires, and we prioritize the spiritual realm within us.

There are many times in the Bible when fasting occurs for a specific reason. In the Old Testament, people fasted because of private problems. For instance, Hannah fasted because she was barren. Sometimes in the Old Testament they fasted because of public disasters, sometimes because of personal grief. Sometimes in perplexity over a situation, sometimes because of a peril that was ahead.

Sometimes fasting took place in penitence over sin. Sometimes because of pity for friends. Sometimes in perplexity over the will of God. The New Testament teaches that certain demons could not be cast out except by prayer and fasting.

I haven't told you all this because I want you to start fasting. The point is that fasting is simply one measure indicating fervency in our relationship with God. I don't believe God is enamored with any emotionless, uninvolved relationship with Him.

Edgar Young Mullins gives an illustration to this point. A little monkey got loose from the organ grinder in the cold wintertime. He was freezing to death and sought warmth. He jumped on the sill of a house and looked through the window pane and saw a roaring fire. He found his way inside the room and sat there with his little paws raised to the fire, but froze to death. The fire was only painted on a screen.

How many churches are like that? How many Christians are like that—fires painted on screens? With no emotion, no fervency, and no warmth? I wonder if we really believe what we say we believe if we're not willing to get involved. When we pray, we need to pray fervently. Read God's Word and see what God wants you to pray about. Then get involved frequently and fervently in talking to your God.

APPLICATION

1. The prayer of Daniel in the ninth chapter is on a par with two other great prayers in the Bible. Read the following:

Matthew 6:9-13

John 17:1-26

There is not a great deal of exhortation and instruction on praying in the Bible. Instead there are prayers that show us how we ought to pray. What principles of praying can you glean from the two preceding passages of prayer?

2. Prayer is always around when the Word of God is being read and understood before the people. Read Ezra 9:1-15.

What is the situation?

What do you think it means in verse four by the statement, "Everyone who trembled at the words of the God of Israel assembled to me"?

Read Ezra 10:1. What were all the things Ezra was doing that were involved in his praying?

Read Ezra 10:2-5. What effect did Ezra's praying have on the people?

Another illustration of dynamic prayer motivated by the Word of God is seen in Nehemiah 8 and 9. What kind of prayer is inspired here?

3. Read 1 John 5:14-15. What does this say about spending time trying to discern from revelation what the will of God is?

If the purpose of prayer is not to get God to change His will, what is the purpose of it?

Think of the last few times you prayed. What was the essence of your prayers? Looking at them now, do you think your prayers were aimed at changing the will of God?

4. Read Daniel 9:20-21. What happened while Daniel was praying?

God is still committed to our being involved in prayer on a frequent basis. Read the following verses:

Luke 18:1

Acts 1:14

Acts 2:42

Acts 6:4

Romans 12:12

1 Thessalonians 5:17

5. Read James 5:16. What does it mean to be fervent in prayer?

In the following verses, what are the causes of fasting?

1 Samuel 1:1-10

1 Samuel 31:1-13

2 Samuel 12:15-23

Esther 4:1-17

Daniel 6:18-20

Matthew 17:14-21

6. What times of crisis, if any, have caused you to be fervent in prayer? How do you express your fervency in prayer?

Do you feel that you express your faith in an emotionless or emotional way? What happens to a relationship that is devoid of emotion?

7. This week, make prayer a priority. Read the Bible and find out what God's revealed will is. Then pray it back to Him. Focus on praying frequently and fervently. See what happens.

DID YOU KNOW?

Leonard Ravenhill has written that the Cinderella of the church today is the prayer meeting. He said, "This handmaid of the Lord is unloved and unwooed because she is not dripping with intellectualism, nor glamorous with the skills of philosophy. Neither is she enchanting with the tiara of psychology. She wears the homespun of sincerity and humility, and is not afraid to kneel." He went on to write that as poverty-stricken as the church is today in many things, she is most stricken here in the place of prayer.

Turning Point Ministries
Resource Books

By Dr. David Jeremiah

The Handwriting on the Wall:
Secrets from the Prophecies of Daniel
   Daniel, divinely inspired, accurately prophesied the rise and fall of empires and their rulers. We cannot pass Daniel off as just the man in the lion's den or the "dreamer." To know Daniel is to know how to live today and look into the future with confidence.
HOW BK $12

ORDER 1-800-947-1993

Escape the
Coming Night:
The Bright Hope of Revelation
Let Dr. David Jeremiah be your guide through the terrifying heights and unfathomable depths of the Book of Revelation. Arm yourself with prophetic truth about things to come so you can live every moment for God, because the end is so clear.
REV BK $10

Acts of Love:
The Power of
Encouragement
   Learn about God's special kind of love for each of us and its power over envy, pride, selfishness, anger, and resentment. Experience Him more fully in your life, your family, and your church as we reflect upon God's Word and His unfailing love.
POE HBK (Hardbook) $18

SEE NEXT PAGE

OTHER STUDY GUIDES & BOOKS
AVAILABLE THROUGH TURNING POINT

Audio cassette albums are also available. For information use our toll-free number.

SELECTION	CODE	QTY	PRICE	TOTAL
Escape the Coming Night—Messages from Revelation				
Revelation Study Guide, 4 volume package	REVSTP	____	$25.	$____
Revelation Study Guide, Volume 1 only	REVSG1	____	$ 8.	____
Revelation Study Guide, Volume 2 only	REVSG2	____	$ 8.	____
Revelation Study Guide, Volume 3 only	REVSG3	____	$ 8.	____
Revelation Study Guide, Volume 4 only	REVSG4	____	$ 8.	____
Acts of Love: The Power of Encouragement Study Guide	POESG	____	$ 8.	____
For Such a Time as This—Esther Study Guide	ESTSG	____	$ 8.	____
Ten Burning Questions from Psalms Study Guide	TBQSG	____	$ 8.	____
Knowing the God You Worship Study Guide	KGWSG	____	$ 8.	____
Seeking Wisdom—Finding Gold Study Guide	WISSG	____	$ 8.	____
Turning Toward Integrity—A Study of James (Book with Study Guide)	TTIBK	____	$10.	____
Turning Toward Joy—A Study of Philippians (Book with Study Guide)	TTJBK	____	$10.	____
Turning Toward Freedom—A Study of Galatians (Book with Study Guide available Summer 1995)	TTFBK	____	$10.	____

BOOKS

The Handwriting on the Wall: Secrets from the Prophecies of Daniel	HOW BK	____	$12.	____
Escape the Coming Night: The Bright Hope of Revelation	REV BK	____	$10.	____
Acts of Love: The Power of Encouragement	POE HBK	____	$18.	____

For Information and
Visa or MasterCard
Orders Call:

1-800-947-1993

$10 minimum for credit card orders.

POSTAGE AND HANDLING CHART

For Orders	Add
Up to $19.99	$1.50
$20.00-$50.99	$3.00
$51.00-$99.99	$6.00
$100.00 & over	$9.00

MERCHANDISE TOTAL	____
SHIPPING/HANDLING	____
SUBTOTAL	____
CA RESIDENTS ONLY ADD 7.75% TAX	____
TOTAL	$____

Please enclose payment with order. Make check or money order payable to:

TURNING POINT • P.O. Box 3838 • San Diego, CA 92163-1838 *(Please allow 4-6 weeks for delivery.)*

Mr/Mrs/Miss _____

Address _____

City/State/Zip _____